DAPHNE MORE

Discovering
Country
Winemaking

SHIRE PUBLICATIONS LTD

Contents

The cover design is by Ron Shaddock

Fig. 1. *Elderberries.
Four recipes for
elderberry wine are
given in this book.*

*Published in 1996 by Shire Publications Ltd, Cromwell House, Church
Street, Princes Risborough, Buckinghamshire HP27 9AA, UK.
Copyright © 1980 by Daphne More. First published 1980, reprinted
1986 and 1996. Number 249 in the Discovering series. ISBN 0 85263
480 3.*

Printed in Great Britain by CIT Printing Services, Press Buildings,
Merlins Bridge, Haverfordwest, Pembrokeshire SA61 1XF.

Introduction

For hundreds of years making wine was a normal part of domestic economy in rural Britain, as was the brewing of beer and, in certain areas, cider. Brewing may have been confined to the farms and larger households but every cottage housewife, however limited her resources, could offer visitors a choice of wines made from garden surplus or hedgerow plants. The materials were all around: gorse and dandelions, elderflowers and berries, cowslips and crab apples. A glut of garden produce, be it gooseberries or parsnips or an abundance of parsley in the herb bed, could be turned into wines of varied flavours.

One hears it said that home-made wine all tastes the same. Nothing could be further from the truth. It is indeed quite difficult to achieve exactly the same result twice, even following the same recipe. This is because seasonal differences, the weather, the ripeness of flower or fruit, its acid or sugar content and the speed of fermentation all affect the final flavour. When one considers that the carefully controlled processes by which French wines are produced give different results from year to year and a superlative result in a vintage year, it is not surprising that our home-made wines show a similar variation. It also adds interest.

Another common complaint is that country wines are too sweet. Traditional recipes do tend to yield sweet wines, for several reasons. The process was not so well understood and too much sugar was sometimes added in an attempt to boost the alcoholic content, leaving a surplus when fermentation ceased. Then the normal diet of country people was deficient in sugar, and sweet things were regarded as luxuries for special occasions, so sweet wines were valued. Certainly a sweet wine was more appropriate for the sort of social occasion when it was drunk. It was the drink offered with a slice of cake to any casual caller, before the ubiquitous teapot took over. It was not so much drunk with food as after the evening meal by the fireside, perhaps with nuts or apples, and probably mulled on cold nights. However it is simple enough to produce dry table wines more in line with today's taste and the advantage of making your own is that you can suit your own palate. Taste is a subjective matter: the same wine may seem to two different people to be delicious or sickly, pleasantly dry or very thin and acid. So make what *you* like.

There are other advantages. One is cost. With care, and a small outlay of money on equipment and materials, you can produce an abundance of wholesome and delicious wines to drink with meals, to share with friends and to cook with if you enjoy continental dishes. You need not live in the country. If you have a garden or allotment you will have access to suitable materials but towndwellers can also take advantage of a glut to buy cheaply from shops and markets or, on a day out in the country, can look out for pick-your-own fruit farms, notices on garden gates offering surplus for sale, or wild blossom or fruit at roadsides. The idea that winemaking needs a lot of space seems to have sprung from Victorian recipes, such as one I have which begins: 'Put 35 pounds of sugar to 10 gallons of water and the well beaten whites of 12 eggs, and let this boil gently for an hour.' What in, one may well ask? Homes and households are smaller today, but so is equipment. Two or three gallons of wine can be made quite conveniently even in a modern flat, as they were in really tiny country cottages in the past. You may find it hard to stop at that ...

Then, in these days of food additives, preservatives, stabilisers and assorted chemicals, you know exactly what goes into your own wine. Many country people claim that some of these wines are beneficial to health. I do not know whether that is so, but it may well be. I do think that they cannot be harmful, drunk in moderation, unless you believe that any consumption of alcohol is harmful, in which case you would hardly be reading this book. Again, we are often told of the need for interesting leisure activities to counteract stressful lives and when retirement brings often unwelcome spare time: here is one with a really worthwhile end product.

My own approach to winemaking is traditional and practical. It is an enjoyable and creative domestic activity, akin to jam making. For this reason I am surprised by the mystique which has grown up around the subject and by the countless wine circles and winemaking guilds which now exist. No one organises jam circles! For centuries there have been wine snobs talking pretentious rubbish on the subject but now home wine-making has become a cult and in some quarters is taken very seriously. I think it is a pity. Indeed, I would find it difficult to be so solemn about anything which I once knew as a bag of fruit and a bucket of water, however satisfactory its transformation.

This book is about the country wines which I have made for years and which my mother, aunts, grandmother, and doubtless a number of 'greats', made before me. The ingredients are the same although quantities have been adjusted and methods streamlined. Today home-made wine is taken to include imitation French wines such as Beaujolais and Sauterne made from kits and concentrates. I have never tried these and they are not covered in this book. The recipes given have come from many different sources: some are traditional in my family;

some were modernised from old books; many were handed on by friends and sometimes strangers; others appear in hand-written recipe books which have been acquired over the years. My old-fashioned thrift decrees that I should not buy materials for winemaking. For wine one uses the surplus which one grows, the free harvest of hedge and field, or possibly the oranges which tumble off a lorry at one's feet. I have never felt tempted to buy apricots for winemaking or to grow turnips, which I dislike, on the chance that a palatable wine might be made from them. The main thing is that you should not regard the recipes as some kind of holy writ. I have explained alternative methods, suggested variations on basic ingredients, but I have left the decisions to you. Half the fun of winemaking lies in experimenting, adapting recipes to suit your taste and the materials available to you, so be adventurous.

Some explanation is needed with regard to quantities. In old recipes these tended to be pecks and bushels or such obscure units of measurement as a pottle, a handful or even 'as much as will go on a penny piece' (of whose reign, one asks oneself). Over the years these were simplified into pints, pounds and ounces, and then metrication loomed on the horizon. As I write, we have reached a state where greengrocers look aghast if a customer wants a kilo of plums, but most jars and packets (and kitchen scales) carry both imperial and metric measures. I have therefore given both, but it is wise to use one set or the other, not a mixture. Mathematicians may notice that the quantities are not exact equivalents but have been rounded up or down a little for the sake of simplicity, where it will hardly affect the result.

Most measurements in winemaking cannot be exact (con-trary to the opinion of some 'scientific' winemakers) because the ingredients are in themselves variable. One pound of plums may have a quite different acid and sugar content from another pound of plums and this will affect the outcome quite as much as putting in a few fruits more or less. Even if the cup is standard, a cupful of strong tea will vary because people's opinions as to what is strong are different, and even the water used affects the strength. The most constant ingredient is likely to be the sugar, and this is best measured accurately once you have decided what amount suits your palate. Even here, the sweetness of any fruit used must be taken into account. There is always an element of guesswork in winemaking. Where table-spoonfuls and teaspoonfuls are mentioned, use an average spoon, reasonably rounded; and use a sensible cup to measure the tea, neither Granny's daintiest nor Dad's jumbo size.

Finally a word of warning: these wines commonly have an alcoholic content of about 15 per cent by volume, which is about 26 degrees proof spirit, and it may be more. (Some commercial wines are as low as 9 per cent.) However pleasant and innocuous they seem, they are not suitable for children to drink and should be treated with respect by adults. They register on the breathalyser like any other alcohol. I have heard that a man who celebrated his birthday too enthusiastically in his own wine showed the effect in a blood test thirty-six hours later. It is illegal to sell them, even at village sales of work or church bazaars, without a licence, which you would be unlikely to get. I understand they can be offered as raffle prizes, although the position should a child win the raffle is not at all clear.

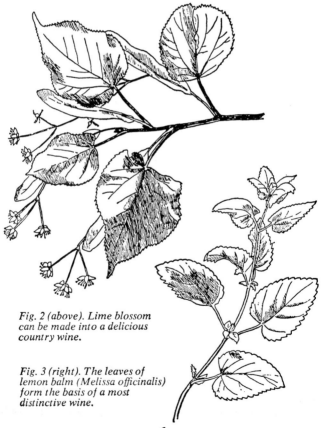

Fig. 2 (above). Lime blossom can be made into a delicious country wine.

Fig. 3 (right). The leaves of lemon balm (Melissa officinalis) form the basis of a most distinctive wine.

1. What is wine?

To the purist, wine is fermented grape juice and nothing else. For country winemaking, the juice may derive from any number of flowers and leaves as well as fruits, which in the British climate will need added sugar. Essentially, wine is the alcoholic drink which results from fermenting this sweet juice, and the process begins with yeast. So yeast is important and we need to understand what it does.

Yeast is a microscopic single-celled organism which multiplies very rapidly, given certain conditions of warmth and moisture. As it multiplies it breaks down sugar, converting it into alcohol and carbon dioxide. This process is the fermentation which produces wine. The carbon dioxide gas escapes as bubbles and is responsible for blowing out corks if the wine is bottled before fermentation ceases. (In bread, the same gas makes the dough rise.) Temperature is crucial: cold retards the development of the yeast and too much heat kills it, so the medium must be kept at a constantly lukewarm temperature, about 16–21 Centigrade (60–70 Fahrenheit).

Wild yeasts are present everywhere. The bloom on a grape or plum skin, for instance, is wild yeast. Many old recipes depend on this wild yeast, and so do the misnamed 'no yeast' recipes given in some modern books. Sometimes the results are fine but often they are not, so it is better to add yeast rather than leave quite so much to chance.

Yeast, water, sugar and warmth are therefore the basics of our winemaking. The flavour, the aroma or 'bouquet' and the 'body' of the wine, as well as some acid, tannin and organic material, are contributed by fruit, cereals, vegetables, flowers, herbs and spices, separately or in various combinations. The flavoured fermenting liquid is called *must*. Fermentation may last for a few weeks or a few months depending on several factors. One is the quantity of sugar in the recipe, which the yeast has available to turn into alcohol. There is a limit to this because when the alcoholic content reaches a certain percentage (about 15 per cent by volume, which means a little over 26 degrees proof spirit) it destroys the yeast and fermentation stops. There may also be a high proportion of natural sugar in the fruit used, causing the must to ferment longer than expected, and temperature changes may accelerate or slow the process. Usually there is a very vigorous fermentation for one to two weeks, then it settles down to a steadier tempo for perhaps two months. The process of making wine is not finished when fermentation ceases. Tasted at this stage the liquid is often quite nasty, and it may be far from attractive in appearance, probably cloudy and a dull colour. Time will change this. As it matures, clears and settles, it becomes a brilliant translucent wine of excellent flavour.

Sometimes a sudden drop in temperature will actually halt fermentation long before it is expected or desirable. This may result in an oversweet wine, as too much sugar is left unconverted when fermentation ceases prematurely. If wine is bottled at this stage, later warmth may revive the dormant yeast, giving a second fermentation and perhaps, if one is lucky, a sparkling or semi-sparkling wine. This is roughly the way champagne is made. If one is less lucky, it can mean blown corks or burst bottles and loss of the wine!

While fermentation is taking place the must needs to be kept securely covered from the air, while provision is made for the gas to escape. The smell attracts flies, particularly the small fruit flies which can infest a kitchen, drown in the fluid and generally make themselves unwelcome. They are fairly harmless in themselves but may carry harmful bacteria. Among these is the invisible but much more serious pest *Mycoderma aceti*, the 'vinegar bug', which can spoil a whole batch of wine by converting the alcohol in the mixture to acetic acid, or vinegar. This is why it is essential to sterilise jars and bottles and to keep spills mopped up and cloths rinsed. Cleanliness is of great importance.

Other things can cause contamination and 'off' flavours in country wines. Using metal containers for fermentation results in a metallic flavour and even, in some cases, toxic substances being absorbed into the wine. Certain old glazed earthenware containers can also release lead and possibly cause poisoning. These are best avoided, however picturesque they look. Old barrels are also suspect, especially those which have held vinegar, and they are not easy to sterilise. In the past many cottagers started their wine in the same copper in which the weekly wash was carried out, since it would be the largest container available. The effect of aged soapsuds and quite probably toxic copper in the wine cannot have enhanced its flavour or healthgiving properties. Other odd flavours can result from faults in the production, like leaving the wine too long on its lees: such mistakes are dealt with in detail elsewhere.

The amount of sugar in the must controls the type of wine, i.e. sweet or dry, and to some extent the alcoholic content. About 2½ pounds (1.1 kilograms) of sugar to one gallon (4.5 litres) of wine will produce the maximum alcoholic content if the fermentation is satisfactory and it is all converted. The wine will then be dry. Any further sugar will be unconverted and so will sweeten the wine, but anything over 4 pounds (1.8 kilograms) to the gallon (4.5 litres) is too sweet for almost any taste. Some allowance must be made for the sugar content of any fruit used and for any added ingredients. The addition of 1 pound (450 grams) of sultanas would represent some 6 ounces (170 grams) of extra sugar, for instance.

Old recipes often suggest adding brandy or other spirits to country wines. In her diary one eighteenth-century housewife records large quantities of brandy added to everything from mead to 'primmy rose' wine: one can only guess that she was on friendly terms with local smugglers! The vinegar bug cannot work when the alcoholic content is higher than is normal in home-made wines, so the added spirit acted as a preservative as well as making the wine stronger by fortifying it. (Sherry and port are commercial fortified wines.) The spirit would be added after fermentation ceased naturally. Added at an earlier stage, it would kill the yeast and at once arrest fermentation, leaving some proportion of the sugar unconverted and the wine sweeter than intended. Added later it would, by killing any remaining yeast, ensure that no secondary fermentation could occur.

Here we should deal with some terms used in winemaking. *Body* is perhaps hardest to explain, though it is obvious to the palate if you taste a light dry table wine and then a robust port. It is a richness, a fullness of flavour. Some fruits naturally give more body to country wines, but where it is likely to be lacking the body of the wine can be improved by adding such things as bananas or raisins to the initial soak. *Bouquet* is the aroma of the wine and should always be fresh and appetising with no hint of mustiness. Elderflower wine, for instance, has a very pleasant natural bouquet; some others have virtually none. Adding something like wallflowers or rose petals at the infusion stage can make good the deficiency but suitability must be considered. A wine with a delicate bouquet and a robust flavour quite at variance with it can be a disconcerting experience.

The *must*, the fermenting liquid, we have dealt with. The *lees* are the sediments which settle to the bottom of the jar and are left behind when the wine is *racked* or siphoned into a fresh jar. They are made up of dead yeast cells and minute particles of fruit and organic matter.

2. Equipment for winemaking

Winemaking equipment can be as extensive as the scale of operations demands. At one extreme it could include fruit presses and steam juice extractors and mechanical corkers; at the other little more than the utensils found in an average kitchen. Homes today are small and I am writing for beginners ın the art of making country wines, so we shall keep to the simple essentials. Later, as experience grows, other equipment can be acquired if it is wanted. Mail-order firms supplying home winemakers send out very extensive lists of equipment, as well as chemicals and concentrates, but do not be alarmed. Everything you need at the start can usually be obtained locally and, as packing and carriage charges are high, this is far the cheapest way. Many local chemists stock equipment for winemaking and branches of Boots carry a good selection, as well as many department stores, hobby and do-it-yourself shops. Consult the Yellow Pages under 'Winemaking supplies' for addresses of specialist shops in your area.

Plastic bucket for soaking

This needs to be large enough to hold the material being soaked as well as one gallon (4.5 litres) of water. Avoid the strongly coloured plastic containers which can contain toxic substances and choose white polythene. Various types are made specifically for the purpose, some with handles attached low at the sides allowing a cloth to be tied neatly over the top to exclude flies and so on. If it is likely to be a nuisance, the handle is easily removed from an ordinary bucket. A second bucket is useful, not only because infusions may overlap at a busy season but so that the juice can be strained from the fruit into it. Keep buckets exclusively for winemaking. However well it is washed, a bucket used for domestic purposes will retain traces of disinfectant or detergent which can taint the wine. Metal containers and old earthenware crocks, as already explained, are best avoided. Old wooden tubs are difficult to clean and tend to leak.

Cloths to cover

Several of these are needed because if one accidentally dips into the liquid it must be replaced at once with a fresh one, rinsed and dried. Fairly thick material is best, such as tea towels or squares of old flannelette sheeting. Some people tie or stitch weights to the corners of these cloths (large metal washers or nuts, for instance) to hold them taut. A string can be tied round the bucket instead but the contents must be stirred daily, and tying and untying this can be tedious. Polythene sheet, not too thick and stiff, can be used if securely fastened.

Stirring spoons

A wooden, not a metal, spoon is needed to stir and press the soaking fruit. Buy a long one, and it needs to be strong, too. An old-fashioned wooden potato masher is a useful implement for crushing fruits, especially the harder ones like apples.

Preserving pan

Some recipes call for boiling vegetables and for this a large saucepan is needed. It can be of aluminium, stainless steel or unchipped enamel. Boiling water is also needed in fairly large amounts but can be heated in two or three instalments if a large pan is not available or is felt to be too heavy or unwieldy.

Fermentation vessel

This must not be of metal. Glass one gallon (4.5 litre) jars are most commonly used and are very convenient, being readily available, easy to clean and sterilise, easily fitted with fermentation airlocks, and easy to move and store. It is also possible to watch the progress of the fermentation. I do not care for old stone jars, though I recognise their nostalgic appeal, because it is impossible to see whether they are really clean or what is going on inside them, quite apart from the possibility of toxic glazes. Sometimes one finds a source of 'useful' containers for wine in the shape of large jars and plastic cans. It is essential to discover what they contained before. I have some glass jars which have never lost their taint of pickled onions. Others may have been used for vinegar, shampoo, salad cream, even weedkillers or insecticides. I would only use those which previously held concentrated squashes and which are sometimes obtainable from snack bars and public houses, although they will probably be superseded by plastic cans before long. I am wary of plastic containers for storage as plastic does absorb smells and flavours and there are well authenticated cases of wines affected by things like floor polish and stored onions, although sealed in plastic containers. If you can find some, it is useful to have one or two half-sized glass jars to make smaller quantities of something very special or for which materials are limited, such as rose-petal wine. The enthusiast may later want to make wine in larger batches, but in the beginning a gallon (4.5 litres) is most convenient, and in the event of a failure the loss is not so costly.

Funnel

This is needed to transfer the juice to the fermentation jar and should be of white or clear polythene and large; about 7 inches (180 mm) across the top is a reasonable size. Smaller funnels are messy and irritating.

Straining cloths

Muslin is good but fine-meshed nylon and Terylene netting can be used and is much easier to rinse clean.

Fermentation airlock

These are of various patterns but all do the same job, which is

11

letting the gas escape from the must through a water trap, which prevents the entrance of harmful bacteria. The glass ones are attractive but easily snapped; plastic ones are less vulnerable. The cylindrical plastic type is the easiest to clean. Bits of dry scum sometimes become lodged in the convolutions of the tubes and can be awkward to remove, though pipecleaners are a help. I made wine for years by putting over the jar necks tiny plastic bags held by elastic bands. The gas is able to force its way out round the neck and the pressure prevents harmful bacteria from entering. Except when the device was accidentally brushed off in passing and not noticed, this worked sucessfully, but proper

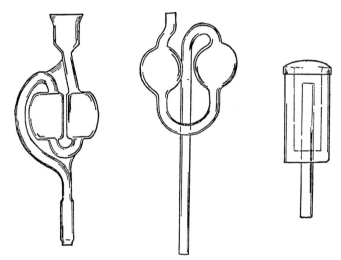

Fig. 4. Types of fermentation airlock.

fermentation locks are so cheap and efficient it is far less bother to use them. Another advantage is that the airlock, by forcing the yeast to get its oxygen needs from the sugar rather than the outside air, causes more sugar to be broken down, so producing a little more alcohol.

Corks

Three types of cork are needed. The first is the big cork which fits the neck of the jar and is pierced to take the stem of the fermentation lock. Secondly, you need an unpierced cork of the same size to close the jar when fermentation is complete and the wine is put away to mature. There are rubber bungs, both pierced and unpierced, to fit standard jars but I find them very rigid and difficult to use, and especially hard to remove after a jar has been stored for a while. Also the necks of my non-standard former orange-squash jars are a fraction smaller and will not take a rubber stopper, whereas the cork type, softened in hot water, will adapt itself to fit. The third type of cork is the one for use in the wine bottle. These should be new and of smooth fine material, not porous or rough. I am old-fashioned enough to prefer the straight cork which fits right into the neck and must be withdrawn with a corkscrew (and a flourish!). Flanged, T-shaped corks are also available and are usually obligatory for shows as they are less trouble for the judge or steward to remove and replace. Plastic flanged 'corks' are new. I have not used them but they have an advantage in that they can be sterilised and reused. They are recommended for use with fortified wines as it is believed the high content of alcohol could dissolve a little of the natural cork, though commercial sherry and so on is still put into bottles with natural corks. For storage, bottles with flanged corks need additional airtight caps over them. These come in a liquid, are put on wet and tighten as they dry out. Do not confuse these with the decorative foil caps which are only for appearance. Once sealed in this way, bottles may be stored upright, while those with straight corks should be stored horizontally.

Corkers

Corks, when they have been soaked in hot water, are soft

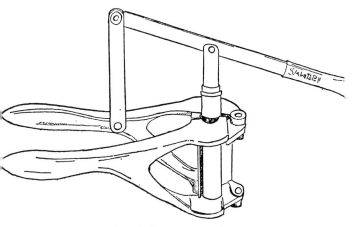

Fig. 5. Lever-type corker.

enough to be worked into the bottle neck by hand to about half their depth. They can be forced in the rest of the way if the bottle is held with the cork against the wall and pushed hard. Many people pound the corks in with a mallet and one man I know uses a cricket bat. These methods result in broken bottles from time to time and something more efficient is advisable. Various implements are available. One is the corking gun, which consists of a hardwood cylinder containing a piston which is tapped on top with a mallet and forces the cork through a slightly smaller aperture into the neck of the bottle. It is essential to hold the corker, not the neck of the bottle, while doing this, in case of breakage. I find the hand-lever type of machine the most satisfactory. The cork is squeezed between two shaped jaws to compress it, positioned over the bottle neck, and then by pressing down a lever is forced into the aperture.

Wine bottles

These can be bought new but it should not be necessary. If you and your friends cannot save enough from bought wines, approach a hotel or restaurant. They only put them in the dustbin and will probably be glad to put them into cardboard cartons for you to collect. Off-licences often receive back empty wine bottles with the returnable beer bottles and will let you take them. Ask friends to rinse their bottles as soon as they are empty as long-dry sediment can be hard to shift. Once you have built up a stock of bottles you will reuse them many times. Do not use thin-walled bottles, such as whisky bottles, or any screw-topped kind, as wine is not stable enough and they could explode. Avoid the kind of bottle with a small neck and a crown cap, but there are several shapes which can be used so long as they will take a standard cork. These include the standard shouldered bottle and the more sloping kind, both with a punt (the internal hump in the base), and the tall narrow hock-type bottle without a punt. They may be clear, faintly green, deep green or brown in colour. It is customary to put red wines in dark bottles and white in clear ones but this is discussed more fully in chapter 7. Half bottles are very useful but scarcer. I prefer to put a jar of wine into five bottles and two half bottles, rather than the normal six, so that I can open a half bottle to sample an untasted batch. If not at its best, it can be used in cooking and I have not sacrificed a whole bottle. They are also handy if I want a glass of wine with a meal when alone or wish to serve different wines with different courses when entertaining. There are a few more litre bottles about now. If the necks are a standard size you can use them. Your jar of wine will fill four litre bottles and one half-litre bottle, leaving a drop over to drink at once or put into the coq au vin.

Bottle brushes

These facilitate cleaning bottles and prevent a lot of annoyance. There are also shaped brushes made especially to reach that awkward area under the shoulder of a fermentation jar.

Siphon

To transfer the wine to the bottles from the jar, a tube is used so that the wine can be siphoned off without disturbing the lees. This may be of rubber or plastic. I like the clear plastic sort as it is stiffer, and so less likely to kink or flatten, one can see the wine passing through it, and it will not perish. About $\frac{1}{4}$ inch (6 millimetres) diameter is fine and some 6 feet (2 metres) will be long enough. You can buy siphons with tubing attached to a rigid J-shaped glass (very liable to breakage) or to a plastic tube which goes into the jar. If the opening is not right at the bottom of the jar, the lees are less likely to be sucked up. For this reason a flexible tube should not be lowered quite to the bottom of the jar. More positive is the home-made device in figure 8. This is a thin wooden lath about 1 inch by $\frac{1}{8}$ inch by 16 inches long (25 millimetres by 3 millimetres by 400 millimetres) to which a length of plastic tube is taped in three places, arranging that it ends about 1 inch (25 millimetres) above the bottom of the lath. This works very satisfactorily. Taps can be bought to close the tube but it is simpler to put one's finger over its end.

Labels and caps

For a neat finish to a good bottle of wine you may like to use a decorative label with the variety and date written in the space provided, and a foil cap of gold, silver or a colour to cover the cork. This looks attractive when a bottle is given away as a present but is wasteful if the wine will be drunk at home, especially when it will be served from a decanter. A small plain label such as is used on pots of home-made jam is sufficient to identify date and variety. The jar also should be labelled with variety and date of starting ferment, racking and so on. It may not matter with the first jar but when you have several bubbling away, confusion is all too easy. I have small tie-on labels for this, and I write in pencil so that they can be reused.

Other utensils and equipment

Many winemaking essentials will already be in the home, for instance a colander for straining. Scales are needed for weighing ingredients and are best if they show both metric and imperial quantities. A glass or plastic jug marked with both pints and litres is often useful, so is a glass or plastic lemon squeezer for juice extraction, and a chopping board and stainless steel knives are necessary for cutting up vegetables and fruit. Though it can be done by hand, many people like to use a mincer to chop dried fruit. I find several of the cheap round tin trays used in public houses useful to stand jars on during the first few days when the ferment may be violent and spills occur. Cotton wool is often useful as a temporary plug for a jar while rinsing the fermentation lock or while making a starter in a bottle (of which more later). Use the plain kind, not medicated, for this.

Wine notebook

It is very frustrating to produce a superlative batch of, say, apple wine and then be unable to remember which of several recipes you used, and the problem is still more trying when you adapt a recipe or make up one of your own and then cannot recall the details, so do keep a record. It will help you repeat a success or do better another time. Perhaps a little more or less sugar would improve a wine? It also helps pinpoint the fault which produced a disappointing result, since the record will show that the ferment was sluggish or that the wine was left too long before racking off. It is up to you whether you do it in columns or take a page for the progress of each brew, but you need to note the variety, method and recipe used, length of soak, any alterations you made, dates of starting and ending fermentation, of racking off, of bottling, and – not least – your comments on the final result.

These are the things you need at the beginning and you could go on making wine for the rest of your life without anything else except more jars, bottles and so on. However, you may like to add some of the following later.

Large containers

A glut of windfall apples or the like may incline you to try a larger quantity of wine. A variety of bigger glass and polythene containers are available for both soaking and fermenting 2, 5 or even more gallons at a time (also 12.5 and 25 litre sizes from some firms). I have found a lidded 5 gallon (22.7 litre) bin in white plastic, rather like a small dustbin, useful for doing a larger initial soak (which only lasts a few days) but still prefer the standard jars for fermentation because of the ease of handling. The larger amount of juice can be divided between the jars and with different treatment, i.e. the addition of fruit juice to one, spices and brown sugar to another, and so on, a variety of flavours can be produced. Those with the space and the inclination can invest in new oak casks and large containers to suit their needs, but there is often a problem of handling, and the loss is considerable if anything goes wrong.

Hydrometer

This is a device for measuring the specific gravity of the must at various stages and by this means working out from tables the possible alcoholic content of the wine. It is not necessary for good winemaking and is apt to worry and confuse beginners. In the hands of an experienced winemaker it is a useful tool allowing him to adjust sweetening to his taste and so on, but leave it till later.

Sacrometer

This is not unlike a hydrometer but simpler and measures sugar content, not specific gravity.

Vinometer

This is a gadget which measures fairly accurately the alcoholic strength of the wine. It is not at all necessary but useful for impressing your friends.

Filter units, filter papers, etc.

I have never found it necessary to filter any wine. Well made wine will clear to brilliance of its own accord. Hazes are due to starch or pectin and these faults are dealt with elsewhere in this book. Filtering does not cure these faults and the over-exposure of the wine to the air is harmful. People often resort to filtering to prepare wine for a show, or because they are impatient to drink it as soon as possible, but it is better to let it clear and mature naturally.

Fermenting cupboard

As constant warmth is vital for fermentation, many people keep their jars near a radiator or in the airing cupboard; others convert a chest or cupboard and fit it with a small thermostatically controlled heater. The efficiency of the cabinet can be improved with insulation. One man successfully converted an old refrigerator, which was of course already insulated to a high standard. The heaters and thermostats are available, reasonably priced, from most winemakers' suppliers. As with all electrical equipment, attention should be paid to safety. Electric trays to hold two to four jars are also on sale but I have not used one myself.

Bottle racks

These may be of plastic-coated metal or of wood and metal. The latter can be made to measure for an available space: both are obtainable in units to hold from ten to seventy-two bottles in a horizontal position. A keen do-it-yourselfer could make his own. Others may content themselves with twelve-bottle cardboard cartons with dividers, from the wine store or supermarket. These can be stacked on their sides to a reasonable height but remember that if you are taking bottles from the bottom the whole stack becomes increasingly unstable and you could start a landslide. A batten of wood laid on the ground under the front edge of the carton to give it a slight backward tilt makes the bottles less likely to slide forward. If flanged corks and seals are used, bottles may be stored upright.

3. First steps in winemaking

For a first attempt we need a straightforward recipe. If you are reading this in the early part of the year dandelion wine is a good choice, but first read the paragraph which starts the next chapter. If it is late summer or autumn, try making apple wine because windfalls or smaller and misshapen apples are easily obtained and cheap. The method is similar.

Dandelion wine

dandelion flowers	5 pints	*3 litres*
sugar (granulated)	3 pounds	*1.4 kilograms*
ginger root	1 ounce	*28 grams*
juice of 1 lemon, 1 orange		
yeast, water		

Pick the open dandelion flowers on a sunny day. Loosely fill a tankard or measuring jug to the required level, shaking but not pressing them down. The green sepals do not matter but nip the heads off the stalks and shake out any small insects. Put the flowers in a plastic bucket and add the ginger root, well crushed; boil about 7 pints (4 litres) of water and pour it over them. Stir well, and cover the bucket with a cloth or thin plastic sheet, and tie a string round it, to exclude flies and bacteria. Note the recipe and the date in your record book. Leave the flowers to infuse for a week, stirring once a day. Line a colander with a layer of muslin and strain the liquid from the soggy flowerheads, or you could use a stool and a cloth tied between its legs or a jelly bag. Put the residue in the compost heap if you have one. Meanwhile sterilise your jar ready for use – see the methods explained below (page 27). Fit a fermentation lock into a pierced jar cork. Do not twist the glass kind as they snap very easily. It is often easier if the cork is first softened in hot water or if the fitting is carried out under a running tap. In obstinate cases try a smear of glycerine on the tube. Push it through until about $\frac{1}{2}$ inch (13 millimetres) of the stem protrudes below the cork: this facilitates removal when it is necessary, as it can be pressed gently down on a flat surface to start it.

If you have sterilised your jar in the oven, make sure it is cool enough not to melt your funnel nor to crack when the juice is put into it, but it need not be stone-cold. Indeed a warm jar will help start the fermentation quickly. Insert the funnel into the neck of the jar and pour in the sugar. The funnel should be bone-dry and even then may clog unless it is held loosely in the jar neck so allowing air to escape around the stem. This is impossible if both hands are needed to pour in the strained juice, and the liquid is apt to gulp and splash. Slip the handle of a dessert spoon between funnel and neck so that an air space is left. Do not use a teaspoon, which is likely to fall into the jar as you take out the funnel. Pour the liquid in on to the sugar, and add the fruit juices and the yeast, either an all-purpose wine yeast used according to the directions on the packet or $\frac{1}{2}$ ounce (14 grams) of dried baker's yeast. Stir gently with the handle of your long spoon. The jar should be well filled but not to the brim. If it is needed, add a little boiled water. If this is still warm it will also help to raise the temperature of the must and start the fermentation. Put some cold boiled water into the airlock – it should fill the U of the bubble-type lock and come just above the lower edge of the cap in the cylindrical type, but remember that water evaporates and check the level from time to time. Press the cork firmly into

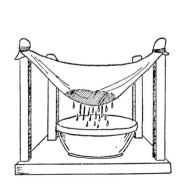

Fig. 6. Straining the juice.

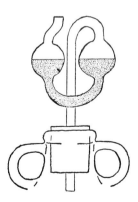

Fig. 7. Filling an airlock.

the jar neck to make sure gas cannot escape around it. Stand the jar on a tin tray if you have one, in a warm place but *not* in direct sunlight. Within hours bubbles will start running up the jar from the bottom and popping out through the airlock. If the fermentation is vigorous at first, froth may pour out. It will soon settle down but in the meantime mop up the mess, take out the airlock (putting in a temporary bung of cotton wool) and rinse it, recharge it with boiled water and replace it. Rinse the cloth you use as well: the smell of must attracts all sorts of flies. If the level of the must has fallen appreciably, top it up a little when the fermentation settles down. It will go on for some weeks. Do not worry if it is working faster or slower or longer than you expect. Many things affect fermentation. If it stops quickly, leaving a quantity of unconverted sugar, or fails to start briskly, the trouble is usually that the temperature is not high enough and is falling during the night and cooling the must so that it is slow to warm up again.

It is worth giving some thought to the question of keeping a constant warmth to encourage a steady ferment. Sometimes a warm place is unsuitable because of the exposure to light, for instance in a sun room or conservatory. Wrapping the jars in thick brown paper to exclude light is quite feasible, and this would incidentally provide some insulation. We can extend this further. Some homes are equipped with central heating which switches off at night and on again in the early morning, which certainly saves energy but adversely affects fermenting wine. I used to wrap all my jars in gingham check tea towels which looked cheerful in the kitchen and helped to maintain a constant temperature within the jar. The wrapping should be loose, not tight, so that a layer of warm air is trapped in between as insulation. More effective is a later improvement on this, in the form of a jacket such as is used to insulate a water tank in many houses. A sleeve is made to fit over the jar with a drawstring to pull tight around the neck. Any material can be used but it is best lined and also interlined with pieces of old blanket or the wadding sold for such a purpose. The best parts of old interlined curtains might be used or ready-quilted nylon can be bought, of the type used for anoraks and dressing gowns. It is advisable to make them of washable fabrics in case of spillage. These jackets may be put on in the evening before the temperature falls and removed in the morning, or they may be left on all the time.

Fermentation has stopped when no more bubbles are leaving the airlock and the liquid is level in the U type. Move or twist the jar and watch to see if any bubbles are released in the bottom of the fluid. It is a good idea to wait a few extra days to make sure. Some wines start to clear before fermentation ceases and others remain cloudy: this is no guide. If you are satisfied that the yeast is exhausted, remove the cork and air-lock, top up the jar with cold boiled water, and put in an ordinary sterilised jar cork.

It may be a good idea to rack off the wine now into another sterilised jar, but unless there is a thick sediment at the bottom it can be postponed for a while. If the wine is already beginning to clear I would leave it a while to continue doing so. When the time comes, the wine is siphoned into a sterilised jar and the sediment left behind. To do this, the top of the empty jar must be below the base of the full one. Stand it on a chair or stool and put the full one on the draining board, or use a chair and the floor. Put one end of the tube well into the full jar. Give the other end a vigorous suck and poke it into the neck of the

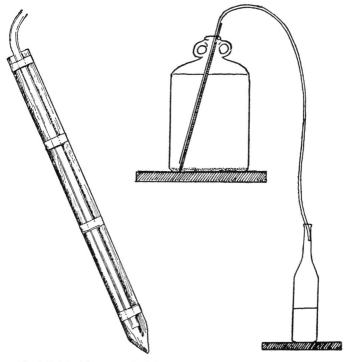

Fig. 8 (left). A home-made siphon.
Fig. 9 (right). Siphoning the wine into bottles.

lower jar as the wine begins to run. You can gently tilt the upper jar as the wine sinks but, if the tube starts to pick up sediment, at once lift it clear of the fluid. If the clean jar is not quite full, top it up with boiled water. The cork needs to be kept wet so that it does not shrink and let in bacteria and air. Push the cork well down and store the jar in a cool dark place, after transferring the label from the discarded jar and recording the date. After three months it may be racked off again if you think there is too much sediment present.

The most difficult task of all now faces the winemaker – leaving the wine alone until it is fit to drink. Any country wine should stay in the jar for at least six months, and dandelion is better for a year. Another three months is advisable after bottling. Do not be in too much of a hurry to bottle any wine as it matures better in the larger container. However, when you do bottle it you will certainly yield to the temptation to taste it. It may be disappointing but do not lose heart and pour it down the sink. After six months in the bottle it may well be superb. I remember some quite unpleasant parsley wine which I kept passing over until, after about two years, I opened a bottle to use in cooking and found it delicious, far too good to cook with.

When the time comes, select six similar bottles or five standard and two half bottles, and sterilise them and sufficient corks. The wine is siphoned into them in exactly the same way as racking off into a fresh jar. Line up the bottles and whip the tube into the next one as the wine reaches to within an inch (25 millimetres) of the top. Let the wine run gently down the inside of the bottle, rather than splashing on to the bottom, to avoid aerating the wine and perhaps starting further fermentation. If you use half bottles, do them last so that if any sediment is picked up at the end it will only affect a small bottle. Do not be tempted to wander away or wash up while bottling wine. The bottles seem to fill very slowly but overflow the second you turn your back, especially the tapered type. Mopping up drinkable wine from the kitchen floor is really heartbreaking. Put in the corks by whatever means you have decided to adopt. If you are using the lever-type corker, pinch the cork between the jaws at a distance and then place it on the bottle neck, otherwise you will squeeze several drops of discoloured water or sterilising fluid straight into the wine. Straight-sided corks should go in to their full depth, and once you are sure no secondary fermentation has started the bottles should be stored on their sides. Flanged corks should be sealed with a plastic cap. These are put on wet and tighten as they dry. Bottles closed this way can be stored upright. All wine should be kept in a cool dark place and not, as often shown in glossy magazine photographs, displayed as part of the kitchen decor, picturesque though it may look.

Apple wine

For the autumn beginner, this is a good wine for the first attempt. Windfalls are fine, but make sure they are clean and cut out any bad bits.

apples, any varieties	4 pounds	*1.8 kilograms*
sugar	3 pounds	*1.4 kilograms*
juice of 2 lemons		
yeast, water		

The method is exactly the same as for the dandelion wine given above. Weigh the apples after preparation. There is no need to peel and core them but they should be cut up into pieces. Pour over them the boiling water and stir well. Soak them for six or seven days, stirring and pressing well daily. Strain off the juice and put it in the jar with the sugar, fruit juice and yeast and proceed as explained above.

This is winemaking at its simplest, and with patience and proper hygiene it will produce a palatable, even excellent, wine. But surely, you may say, there is more to it than that? You may have read recipes in old cookery books which involve leaving the fruit to form a crust of mould on top and spreading yeast on toast to float on the must. The process which produces wine was not really understood then and many unnecessary things were done. Superstition surrounded it also. I have known people who stir the brew with a birch or hazel wand (other places have other preferences) to start the fermentation – which it does not – and folk who believe that when the sap rises in the parent tree, say the hawthorn, the hawthorn wine in your cupboard will sympathetically start to ferment again in its bottles – nothing to do with a spring rise in temperature after the cold winter, of course! Wine was also supposed to be made at certain times according to the phases of the moon but I doubt if success was thereby assured if you failed to exclude the vinegar bug.

What then of all these things in the winemaker's catalogues and displayed on shelves in the shops? Special yeasts and nutrients, tablets and powders which look like patent medicines or insecticides – are they not necessary or at least advisable? In fact, nothing else is essential but in certain circumstances some of these things are helpful and may be convenient. With experience you will recognise what you would find useful, but there is no need to complicate things unnecessarily at the start. There are things on sale for which you will never feel a need.

In an age when everything we eat seems to be saturated with additives, I am reluctant to use any chemicals and will always add a natural substance rather than a powder from a packet if a deficiency needs to be remedied. Country wines should be made from natural ingredients as far as possible. However, with your first jar of wine on its way, it is time to discuss further the ingredients of winemaking and some alternative methods which are available to us.

Water

Old recipes often specify spring water. This is not surprising because at the time the only alternative, well water, often smelled and tasted stagnant and was frequently polluted by dead livestock and badly sited earth closets. Heavily chlorinated urban water supplies can also smell and taste unpleasant although sufficiently sterile for health. Boiling the water dispels chlorine. Some people recommend rainwater. This would be soft, unlike the tapwater in many districts, but apart from the need to filter out insects, rainwater these days is apt to be full of pollutants from industrial concerns, crop spraying and refineries. In remote places rainwater might be usable, and delicious spring water is also available, but only to the few.

Sugar

White granulated sugar is usually used in winemaking but Demerara sugar can be used to give a richer flavour and colour. It is not always appropriate: for instance, I would hesitate to use it for a delicately flavoured rose-petal wine. It is, though, a matter of personal taste. Golden syrup also gives a richer taste but like Demerara it costs more than white sugar. Glucose chips are expensive, too, and seem to have no particular advantages. Honey, unless you keep bees, is also highly priced for winemaking and pound for pound is less sweet than sugar. However, using part sugar and part honey is less prohibitive and can produce something special. Honey contains 20 per cent of water, so recipes need to be adapted a little. Adding dried fruit to a recipe to give the wine more body means adjusting the sugar too. 1 pound (450 grams) of raisins will add 6–8 ounces (170–226 grams) of sugar. Bananas, ripe but not too black and mushy, are usually regarded as about 25–30 per cent sugar.

Spices

Spices added to the wine for flavouring are best put in whole, i.e. ginger root and whole cloves, rather than as ground spices, which can be difficult to strain out. Sometimes they will settle with other sediments, but not always.

Yeast

So far we have used the ordinary dried yeast sold for bread-making, but there are other kinds ranging from the putty-like fresh yeast obtainable from bakeries and always used by country housewives in days gone by, to specially cultivated wine yeasts sold as liquids, powders, tablets and granules. These have the names of world-famous wines like Niersteiner, Liebfrau-milch, Champagne and Tokay, but it is unwise to assume that by using a Tokay yeast you can produce a dandelion wine tasting like Tokay, even supposing you know what Tokay tastes like. As experience grows you will want to experiment with these named yeasts, using a Burgundy yeast for elder-berry, a Sauternes for that sweet white gooseberry wine. These yeasts can tolerate a little more alcohol in the wine before they die and fermentation ceases, so, in theory at least, a slightly stronger wine can be made. One great advantage is that these yeasts form a firmer sediment at the bottom of the jar instead of floating about in the lower levels, so it is easier to rack off the wine without disturbing it. All the firms selling wine yeasts stock an 'all-purpose' one, which would be a good choice for a first trial and may be used with confidence. Do not keep yeast in the cupboard for years. It does deteriorate so buy it more or less as you need it.

Yeast nutrients

These are chemicals such as nitrogen and phosphorus which are intended to stimulate the activity of the yeast and promote brisk fermentation. They are sold as powder or as tablets which have to be crushed before being added to the must. The sub-stances are usually present naturally but if fermentation is sluggish for no obvious reason adding nutrient could help. Follow the instructions on the packet and do not be tempted to use too much. Some wine yeasts are combined with nutrient already, so read what is on the packet.

Acid

Acid helps fermentation and enhances flavour. It is present in most fruits, but flowers, grains and vegetables do not con-tribute any so it should be added when these materials are used for wine. Citric acid is obtainable as crystals to use when acid is lacking but I prefer to add the juice of lemons and oranges (or even rhubarb) as a natural source. The fruit juice blends with the wine and improves the flavour without any of that tang, like commercial lemonade, which one notices if the crystals have been used, perhaps too enthusiastically. Other acids like malic, lactic and succinic acids are sometimes recommended to improve flavour and bouquet but these need time to do their work – two or three years – so do not benefit wines intended for quick consumption. The amount of acid desirable in wine is a matter of taste and it is better to err on the side of too little rather than too much at first.

Tannin

This aid to good fermentation and keeping quality is present naturally in the skins and pips of fruit (elderberries have almost too much) and in such things as oak leaves. Root, grain and flower wines are apt to be deficient in tannin, but the addition of raisins corrects this. Tannin can be bought in powder or liquid form but is available without cost in the bottom of your teapot. One cupful of strong tea (no milk!) is sufficient for a jar of wine. If a little too much is used it does not leave such an astringent tang as an accidental overdose of the bought additive does.

Pectin-degrading enzyme

Under certain circumstances, which are discussed in chapter 5, the pectin present in some fruits may be released into the must. This is the component which makes preserves jell but in wine the glutinous substance causes cloudiness. Pectin-degrading enzyme can be used to avoid this trouble. It is sold under various names such as Pectinol and Pectolase.

Campden tablets

These tablets, which are sulphur dioxide, have become important in home winemaking recently, although wine was made successfully for hundreds of years without them. They are often used to destroy any bacteria or wild yeasts on the fruit in the initial infusion, which can then be done with cold water. One tablet is crushed to a powder between two spoons and dissolved in half a cup of warm water, then stirred into the pulp and water in the bucket. The solution is made up fresh when needed. Again, one tablet is often added as a preservative when the wine has finished fermenting and is sealed for storage. The tablet is dissolved in some wine from the jar and then returned to it, but it must be evenly dispersed throughout the total quantity, so it is best done while racking off the wine. Trying to stir a jarful of wine only leads to spills. But, although the practice is widespread and unobjectionable, I doubt its necessity. Boiling water will destroy harmful organisms in the initial soak and certainly draws out more flavour than does cold water. Using Campden tablets may also inhibit the start of a good fermentation as selected yeast, as well as the wild variety, is affected by them. Indeed, Campden tablets, by effectively destroying any live yeast remaining when the jar is to be closed down, will ensure that no secondary fermentation could start while the wine is being stored. This may be useful, though their use as a preservative should not be taken too seriously. I have never known any wine which was properly made, sealed and stored fail to keep.

Methods of sterilising

The old way to sterilise glass jars and bottles was to put them in a cold oven, put on the heat at its lowest setting and leave it for one hour, then allow to cool. If they are removed while hot, stand them on a board or thick dry tea towel as they will crack if placed on a wet or cold surface. Plug the necks with cotton wool. I still use this method. Corks and straining cloths can be sterilised in boiling water. Spoons and oddments are washed in very hot water without detergent.

Difficulties arise with plastic storage and fermentation vessels which cannot be sterilised by heat. Campden tablets can be used to make a sterilising solution for this kind of equipment. Anything from two to six tablets are recommended, to be dissolved in one pint (570 millilitres) of water, and some people advise adding a teaspoonful of citric acid as well. Campden tablets are virtually the same as sodium metabisulphite, which is sold as a powder in packets. This can be made up as a solution of 2 ounces dissolved in 1 pint of water to which more water is added to make it up to half a gallon (56 grams dissolved in 570 millilitres of water, then made up to 2.5 litres). This can be kept in a stoppered jar and used several times for swilling out bottles and jars. One expert will say the vessel, cork or whatever should be given another quick rinse with cool boiled water immediately before use; others protest that it is totally unnecessary. You must decide for yourself. I would rinse again but I have admitted a phobia about chemicals and their inclusion in what I eat and drink. The packets in which sodium metabisulphite is sold carry a warning about taking the contents internally and keeping them out of the reach of children, so at least do not exceed the concentration recommended by the manufacturer. The fumes from the metabisulphite solution are unpleasant and you should avoid inhaling them, especially if you are an asthma sufferer. I sometimes notice the smell of sulphur from a newly opened bottle of a friend's wine, though it disperses quite quickly, unlike the odd taste which I believe derives from the same source.

Starter bottle

Dried baker's yeast may be added directly to the must and so can the special wine yeasts and tablets, but to get a quicker start the yeast can be activated first. The usual method is to put $\frac{1}{2}$ ounce (14 grams) of chopped raisins and a good teaspoonful of sugar into a bottle (large enough to allow expansion) and add $\frac{1}{4}$ pint (150 millilitres) of hot water. When it is lukewarm, put in the yeast tablet or granules and shake it up. Plug the neck with cotton-wool and put the bottle in a warm place, such as an airing cupboard, for a few hours. It is added to the liquid in the jar once it is working well, so it is usual to prepare the starter twenty-four hours before the juice is strained from the pulp. It is advisable to make sure the jar and its contents are thoroughly warm before the starter is added because sudden immersion in a large quantity of cold liquid will at once check the fermentation.

On-pulp fermentation

So far we have extracted our juice by infusing flowers or chopped fruit in boiling water, then fermenting it in a jar after straining. Another method is to start the fermentation in the bucket by adding a yeast starter or dry yeast when the contents have cooled sufficiently. This may continue for three to seven days, after which the must is strained into a jar and fermented under an airlock. In the past, when fermentation locks were not available, the on-pulp method was customary and the wine was left on the solids often for several weeks. The risk of contamination was greatly increased and so was the likelihood of 'off' flavours arising from the decomposing pulp. However, good wine can be made by fermenting on the pulp for a few days, though in small houses people are happy to see the must safely and tidily in its jar as soon as possible. When this method is used, it is usual to add less water at the beginning, put in part of the sugar with the pulp, and add the remainder in the form of syrup after the must is transferred to a jar. The syrup should be warm, as should the jar, to avoid arresting the fermentation. If all the sugar were added at the start, some would inevitably be absorbed by the pulp and thrown away with it. With fruit wines, the sugar contained in the fruit is often enough to start a satisfactory on-pulp fermentation and all the additional sugar can be added to the jar.

Gradual sugar

As an alternative to adding all the sugar when starting the fermentation in a jar, it may be added in two or three instalments. I have made good wine by both methods and have never noticed any difference, so it is a matter of choice. It is essential to decide before you start the wine which system you mean to follow, because you must not fill the fermentation jar to the top if you intend to add a further quantity of sugar, especially as syrup, i.e. 1 pound (450 grams) dissolved in 1 pint (0.5 litres) of water. It is fatally easy to top up a jar in an absent-minded moment. Make a note of the date and of the amount added as it is easy, when you have several jars of wine all at different stages of their fermentation, to confuse them. I find it helpful to make a note on the jar label as well as in the record book, just to make sure that no wine gets an extra dose while another goes short.

4. Flower and leaf wines

In the past wines were made from a great many wild flowers culled from the road verges, commons and fields of our country-side, but times have changed and you must be careful. People driving in the country assume that all wild flowers are fit to use. *They are not.* Apart from the possible pollution from exhaust fumes, many toxic chemicals are used in the country. Road verges are often sprayed with herbicides and this may not be noticeable in the condition of the plants for a day or two, by which time the poisonous flowers could be in some-one's wine bucket. Herbicides are also used on crops like young corn and may affect hedgerows too. Pesticides are even more widespread, varied and dangerous. Orchard trees are sprayed, sometimes three or four times a year, and one must be wary about picking dandelions growing underneath them. Honeybees visiting orchard dandelions are often killed in thousands. Aerial crop spraying, by helicopter, is far more serious. The crops sprayed by this means include field beans and peas, oilseed rape (those fields of violently yellow flowers one sees increasingly in Britain) and even young trees. The hedges and headlands of the fields are equally polluted, and where adjacent fields are sprayed the spray is often spread across any lanes or roads which intervene. Furthermore, should there be even a slight breeze, spray will drift in a poisonous cloud across private gardens and orchards and smallholdings. I often wonder how many stomach upsets dismissed as 'that tummy-bug (or virus) which is going around' are due to such poisons. Bee-keepers are aware of the extent of the problem but so far the general public is not. I do not want to be too alarmist but I do advise caution.

Not all flowers and leaves are suitable for winemaking. Poppies, buttercups, rhubarb leaves and various others are definitely harmful, so do not experiment with anything which you do not know to be safe. Most herbs used in cooking can be used for wine but some are too pungent. Cowslip wine was a traditional favourite but for conservation reasons should not be made now. Cowslips have become very scarce. Even though the roots are not disturbed, taking the flowers prevents seed being ripened and scattered, so the colony does not renew itself. Primroses too are endangered and where they still exist are better left to flower undisturbed. It is easy to say that many causes contribute to eliminate wild flowers (which is true) and that winemakers will make no difference. After two or three years, in each of which I made three or four jars of dandelion wine, I virtually wiped out dandelions in my large garden and orchard and in the lanes in the immediate vicinity, and for the next few years had to go further afield for them. Windborne seed re-established them and I am not suggesting you restrain yourself from picking dandelions but it shows what effect one person can have on his environment.

Ideally, flowers should be picked when they are well open and as soon as the dew dries off them in the morning, not when they are flagging after the heat of the day and the bees have taken all the nectar. Use them as soon as possible after picking as flowers deteriorate very quickly.

General instructions

To avoid repeating the method for every recipe given, I will go over the basic procedures which are common to all. The process and alternatives are given in detail in chapter 3. For flower wines, the infusion method gives the freshest flavour. Fermentation on the pulp can give an odd taste. Infusion also ensures that the must is safely under an airlock at the earliest moment, thereby cutting down the risk of contamination and releasing the bucket for further use at what is likely to be the busiest season.

Pour on the boiling water and keep the bucket closely covered during the soaking stage. Stir daily. Sterilise the jar and as soon as it is filled fit an airlock. Label the jar. Keep it in a warm place, shielded from light. Mop up any spills as soon as possible. Keep the airlock clean and ensure the water in it does not evaporate. If you wish to add the sugar in instalments, especially as syrup, remember to leave space for it, and keep a note of the date and amount. When fermentation ceases, top up the jar and close with a sterilised cork. Put away in a cool dark place.

In the following recipes no quantities are given for water or yeast. Water is enough for one gallon (4.5 litres) of wine. In practice 7 pints or 4 litres is enough for the initial infusion when all the sugar is to be added at once; 5 pints or 3 litres may suffice at first if the sugar, or part of it, will be added later as syrup. When necessary the jar can be topped up with cool boiled water after all the ingredients have been added. Yeast may be the special wine yeast of your choice used according to the maker's instructions or half of a 1 ounce or 28 gram packet of dried baker's yeast. You need not be too fussy about the amount of yeast: a little more will do no harm although much less might mean a slow start. However, given the right conditions, yeast multiplies at an amazing rate, unless it has been too long in stock and become stale. Whether you add yeast nutrient or not is left to your own discretion.

Where oranges or lemons are included, peel or juice only may be specified. Before using any peel, dunk the fruit several times in a pan of boiling water to destroy any lurking nasties, then rub dry. Slice off the outer rind with a sharp knife or potato peeler, avoiding the bitter white pith.

To measure pints or litres of flowers, fill a beer tankard or measuring jug *loosely*, i.e. shaken but not pressed down, to the required level. For larger quantities a bucket with graduated markings may be used. Except where otherwise stated, the green calyx of, for instance, dandelions need not be removed, nor the tiny stalks of elderflowers, though larger ones should be.

Brambletip wine

This wine is included to show what unlikely material can be used in winemaking.

tips of young blackberry shoots	1 gallon	*4.5 litres*
sugar	3½ pounds	*1.6 kilograms*
yeast, water		

Boil the tips in as much of the water as will go into your pan, the tips being rather bulky, or do them in two parts. Simmer for thirty minutes, then strain off the juice. Put it into the jar with the sugar and add more (boiled) water if necessary. When the liquid has cooled enough, add the yeast and ferment under an airlock in the usual way.

Dandelion dark

This is a sweeter more robust wine than the one for which the recipe is given in chapter 3.

dandelion flowers	5 pints	*3 litres*
raisins	8 ounces	*225 grams*
brown sugar (Demerara)	4 pounds	*1.8 kilograms*
juice of 1 lemon, 1 orange		
yeast, water		

Chop the raisins and put into the bucket with the flowers. Pour on the boiling water. Leave for six days, closely covered, stirring daily. Strain off the liquid and put it into a jar with the sugar, fruit juices and yeast, and ferment under an airlock.

Elderflower wine

Make sure you are using elderflowers: I have heard of people picking other flowers which grow in flat umbels, among them cow parsley and hemlock! The elder is a large bush or small tree, not a hedgerow plant, and has rather dark compound leaves. Do not be tempted, because it is plentiful, to use more blossom than is stated. The perfume is quite strong and has been described with some truth as 'enough, like muscat; too much, like tomcat'. Muscat is the sweet muscatel grape from which wine of the same name is made.

elder blossom	1 pint	*0.5 litres*
sugar	3 pounds	*1.4 kilograms*
crushed whole ginger	1 ounce	*28 grams*
juice of 1 lemon, 1 orange		
yeast, water		

Infuse flowers and ginger in boiling water, stirring daily, for four or five days, then strain. Put the liquid in a jar with the sugar, fruit juices and yeast and ferment as usual.

Elderflower wine II

elder blossom	1 pint	*0.5 litres*
raisins	8 ounces	*225 grams*
brown sugar (Demerara)	3½ pounds	*1.6 kilograms*
6 cloves		
juice of 1 lemon, 1 orange		
yeast, water		

Infuse the flowers with the cloves and chopped raisins for four or five days, stirring daily. Strain off the liquid and ferment with the sugar, fruit juices and yeast under an airlock in the usual way.

Folly wine

This recipe was given me years ago by someone who was quite unable to explain why it has this name. It is made from the young leaves, tendrils and tiny unripe grapes pruned from a grapevine and thinned from the bunches.

vine trimmings	5 pounds	*2.3 kilograms*
sugar	3 pounds	*1.4 kilograms*
yeast, water		

Put the vine shoots and grapes in a bucket and pour over them the boiling water. Cover the bucket and leave for three or four days, stirring and pressing the contents daily. Strain off the liquid, squeezing the prunings well. Put it into a jar with the sugar and yeast and ferment under an airlock as usual.

This makes a pleasant dry wine using $2\frac{1}{4}$ pounds (1 kilogram) of sugar, and a hock wine yeast gives a very good result.

Golden rod wine

golden rod flowers	1 pint	*0.5 litres*
raisins	8 ounces	*225 grams*
sugar	$3\frac{1}{2}$ pounds	*1.5 kilograms*
juice of 4 oranges		
yeast, water		

Infuse the flowers with the chopped raisins for three to four days, then strain off the liquid, put it in a jar with the sugar, orange juice and yeast and ferment as usual.

Lemon balm wine

This wine is known in my family as Melissa because when I first made it I did not know the common name of the herb *Melissa officinalis*. It is an invasive plant in the garden, like mint, and often occurs at roadsides as an escape from cottage plots. The flowers are white and inconspicuous but the plant can always be recognised by the strong lemon smell if a leaf is pinched in the fingers.

lemon balm leaves	3–4 pints	*1.7–2.3 litres*
sugar	3 pounds	*1.4 kilograms*
juice and pared rind of 1 lemon		
yeast, water		

Boil the water with the slivers of rind in it, then pour it over the leaves in the bucket. Soak, giving an occasional stir, for four days, then strain, place in a jar with the sugar, lemon juice and yeast and ferment as usual.

Lime blossom wine

If there is difficulty in obtaining fresh lime flowers, packets of dried ones can be bought. Of these, only 1 ounce (28 grams) is needed for a jar of wine. Some country winemakers dry the fresh blossom in the sun for a few hours before use in the belief that it enhances the flavour.

lime blossoms	3 pints	*1.5 litres*
raisins (chopped)	12 ounces	*350 grams*
sugar	2 pounds	*0.9 kilograms*
clear honey	1 pound	*450 grams*
pared rind of ½ orange		
juice of 1 lemon		
cupful of strong tea		
yeast, water		

All sugar instead of part sugar and part honey may be used if preferred. Put the lime blossoms and the orange peel (no white pith) with the raisins into a saucepan, add the water and bring to the boil. Simmer very gently for fifteen minutes, then tip into the bucket, cover closely and leave for three days before straining. If honey is to be used, it is easiest to dissolve it in hot water before putting it into the jar, so allowance must be made for this by cutting down the water used in the boiling process, or else some of the strained liquid may be reheated and the honey dissolved in that. Put the liquid into the jar with the lemon juice, sugar and dissolved honey if used, add yeast and ferment as usual.

This wine may be drunk after fermentation ceases but is better kept for at least three months. It can also be bottled just before fermentation ceases to give a sparkling wine, but judging this is always a chancy business.

Marigold wine

The old-fashioned 'pot' marigold with single flowers is the one to use for wine. It is one of the flowers which will seed all over a garden if allowed, and one sometimes comes across an abandoned one which is full of them. The green calyx on a marigold flower is large so try to pull the petals from them as far as possible and discard the green part.

marigold petals	4 pints	*2.3 litres*
sugar	3 pounds	*1.4 kilograms*
1 lemon, 2 oranges		
yeast, water		

Peel some of the rind from the lemon and one orange, without taking any white pith, and infuse it with the petals in boiling water for four days, stirring daily. Strain and ferment in a jar with the sugar, juice of the lemon and both oranges, and yeast.

May wine

This is made with may blossom, the flowers of the hawthorn tree.

may blossom	4 pints	*2.3 litres*
sugar	3½ pounds	*1.5 kilograms*
1 orange, 1 lemon		
yeast, water		

Peel the citrus fruits thinly and put the rind into a bucket with the blossom and pour over the boiling water. Leave for four or five days, stirring occasionally, then strain and ferment in a jar with the sugar, fruit juices and yeast.

Mint wine

mint, freshly picked	1 pound	*0.5 kilograms*
ripe bananas	1 pound	*450 grams*
sugar	3 pounds	*1.4 kilograms*
2 lemons		
cupful of strong tea		
yeast, water		

Cut up the bananas, including the skins, which should not be too blackened and should be washed first. Put them in a sauce-pan with the mint and add water. You may not be able to put in all the water you need but this does not matter. Leave some space at the top of the pan as bananas froth up a lot. Bring to the boil and simmer for about thirty minutes. Strain the juice into a bucket, cover it and leave overnight to allow sediment to settle. Siphon or carefully pour off the juice into the jar. Add the sugar, lemon juice, tea and yeast. This often ferments very violently for a few days so delay topping up the jar for a while until you see how it is going, to avoid spillage and waste. Be sure to keep the airlock clean. Thereafter proceed as usual.

This is a strong herby wine, not liked by everyone, but it lends itself to variation in several ways, so experiment with it.

Parsley wine

Use the parsley foliage but remove the main stalks; smaller ones do not matter.

parsley	1 pound	*450 grams*
sultanas	1 pound	*450 grams*
sugar	2½–3 pounds	*1.2–1.4 kilograms*
2 oranges, 2 lemons		
yeast, water		

Grate some of the rind from the oranges and add to the washed parsley in a saucepan. Do not worry if you cannot boil all the water at once but put in as much as you can, bring it to the boil and simmer, covered, for fifteen minutes. Chop the sultanas, put in the bucket and strain over them the boiling liquid from the parsley, squeezing the latter well. After four days, stirring daily, strain out the sultanas and put the liquid in the jar with the juice of the citrus fruits, the sugar and yeast, and ferment as usual. This wine I sometimes ferment for seven days on the solids (sultanas) as the parsley has already been discarded, i.e. the fermentation is begun at once in the bucket with part of the sugar. I think it takes more flavour from the sultanas but the bucket must be kept securely covered.

Parsley wine II

parsley	1 pound	*0.5 litres*
sugar	3 pounds	*1.4 kilograms*
root ginger (crushed)	1 ounce	*28 grams*
2 lemons		
yeast, water		

Boil the parsley in water with the bruised ginger for fifteen minutes as in the previous recipe, then strain and put into a fermenting jar with the sugar, the lemon juice and yeast, and proceed as usual.

Rose-petal wine

This may seem a waste of roses but it is a very delicate wine, and remember how soon the roses drop. You can enjoy them in the middle of winter as you sip your wine. Halve the quantities and try a smaller amount first if you have a suitable jar. Red roses make the prettiest wine but any fragrant variety may be used. Those from the hedging rose, *Rosa rubiginosa*, would do very well. Pick the petals from newly opened and not rain-damaged blooms and use them at once.

rose petals	4 pints	*2.3 litres*
sugar	3 pounds	*1.4 kilograms*
juice of 2 lemons, 1 orange		
yeast, water		

Put the petals into the bucket and pour on the boiling water. Infuse for four days, then strain and put the liquid into a jar with the sugar, fruit juice and yeast, and ferment as usual.

Rose petal wine II

rose petals	5 pints	*2.8 litres*
sugar	2 pounds	*1 kilogram*
clear honey	1 pound	*450 grams*
juice of two lemons		
yeast, water		

Put the petals into a bucket and pour over them 4 pints (2.3 litres) of boiling water. Soak for three days, stirring daily, then strain the liquid into a jar and put the petals into a saucepan with 3½ pints (2 litres) of water. Bring to the boil and simmer for twenty minutes, then dissolve the sugar and honey in the liquid, strain it, and add it to the jar. Add the lemon juice, and when it is cool enough stir in the yeast and ferment as usual.

These recipes are for wines with a predominant flower or leaf flavouring, although some include other ingredients. Mixed flower wines are also a possibility and could be the answer if not enough of one kind is available. A mixture of lime, clover and gorse, which are often in flower at the same time, might well yield an interesting result.

Another use for flowers is as an addition to something else, to contribute more flavour or, particularly, bouquet. Apple and rhubarb are examples of basic wines to which a variety of ingredients may be added to yield a wide range of flavours. The following is a mixed flower and fruit wine.

Wallflower and rhubarb wine

Red wallflowers are most often used, to produce a rosé wine, but yellow flowers are equally good and a mixture of both may be used. The rhubarb should be fairly young. Late-season rhubarb is mostly water and acid with not much taste.

wallflowers	2 pints	*1.4 litres*
rhubarb	4–5 pounds	*1.8–2.3 kilograms*
sugar	3 pounds	*1.4 kilograms*
yeast, water		

Put the flowers in a bucket with the rhubarb cut up in chunks, and pour boiling water over them. Crush, stir and press daily for six days, then strain off the liquid, put it in the jar with the sugar and yeast and ferment as usual. My aunt used to add a glass of brandy to this when it was racked off after completing fermentation, but whether this was to help it keep (as she said) or because she liked it, I am not sure. Like many other home winemakers of days gone by, she regarded herself as teetotal!

5. Fruit wines

Fruit of various kinds is the most popular and diverse material for country wines, whether it be the wild harvest of sloes, elderberries, blackberries and crab apples, or the glut of garden fruit – apples or gooseberries perhaps – which occurs in some favourable years. This sudden abundance of fruit can be overwhelming but if you have a deep freeze you can use it to store fruit for winemaking at a more convenient time.

The warning about hedgerow flowers being contaminated by aerial sprays (chapter 4) also applies to wild fruits. A friend of mine was able to stop a family picking blackberries which he knew had been soaked with insecticides from a helicopter shortly before, but who warned the next people to be tempted by all that free fruit? So please take care.

Fruit should be clean and sound and picked when it is dry and, ideally, warm from the sun. Avoid including leaves and twigs but little stalks do not matter – do not 'top and tail' gooseberries for instance – and nothing needs peeling or coring. Discard mildewed berries and cut out rotten bits from apples and pears. Plum and peach stones should be removed also. Soft berries need to be mashed up in the bucket, using the fingers if you like when the water has cooled. Harder fruits likes apples and rhubarb need to be chopped or cut up, using a stainless steel implement, before going into the bucket, and well crushed and pressed before the water is poured on them. The hardest fruit, the quince, has to be cooked a little. Unfortunately this releases a large amount of pectin, the same thing which makes jelly set, and this persists in wine as a cloudy film, spoiling its appearance although not its taste. This is the time when a pectin degrading enzyme is advisable. The problem may arise when any recipe requiring the boiling of fruit is used, but in most cases cooking is unnecessary and does affect the fresh fruit flavour. Where orange or lemon peel is used, remember to clean it in boiling water first (page 31).

Quantities of fruit given in the following recipes are not crucial. You could use up to 6 pounds (2.7 kilograms) to produce a heavy fruity wine, or as little as 1½ pounds (680 grams) for a light dry table wine. 4 pounds (1.8 kilograms) is an average which is generally acceptable. In a few cases it is a maximum. Elderberries contain so much natural tannin that the result of using more fruit would be a very astringent taste. This would probably moderate if the wine were kept for several years but few winemakers are so patient. Where much natural tannin is present, a long on-pulp fermentation is apt to leach out an undesirable amount so if this method is used limit it to three days before straining. Most fruits have enough natural tannin to ensure a good fermentation so no more need be added.

General instructions

For the infusion method, prepare fruit and pour on the boiling water; stir daily while keeping closely covered. Sterilise a jar, and fit an airlock as soon as it is filled. Label the jar. Keep it in a warm place and shielded from sunlight while must ferments. Mop up spills at once, keep the airlock clean, and check that water does not evaporate from it. If adding sugar in stages, remember to allow space for it, especially if adding it as a syrup, and note down the date and amount. If you want to start the fermentation in the bucket, add yeast or a starter when the water is at the right temperature and put in part of the sugar. When the fermentation ceases, top up the jar, close with a sterilised cork, and store in a cool dark place. Fruit wines often benefit from racking off quite soon and again after six months.

Apple wine

A drier version of the recipe given in chapter 3 can be made using 2 pounds (0.9 kilograms) of sugar. Much depends on the apples used, not only the variety, sweet or sharp, but also whether the fruit is ripe or not. A good mixture of eating apples, cookers and crab apples is probably the best. Crab apples are high in tannin and acid.

Apple is a good basic wine for endless variation, which can be welcome if there is a glut of windfalls. Different wines can be produced with additions of orange juice, rosehip syrup, mint leaves, cloves, ginger, Ribena or dried fruits, or by using apples in various proportions with other fruits which may be scarcer or expensive.

Apricot wine

Apricots are seldom on sale at a low price but may be available if you have a tree. This is a strong fruity wine but less fruit could certainly be used.

apricots	6 pounds	*2.5 kilograms*
sugar	3 pounds	*1.4 kilograms*
juice of 2 lemons		
yeast, water		

Halve the apricots and discard the stones. Pour on the boiling water, mash and stir well. Leave in the bucket for four to six days, keeping it well covered and stirring daily. Strain off the juice and put it in the jar with the lemon juice, sugar and yeast, and ferment to a finish.

I have not used dried apricots myself but I am told that a very pleasant wine can be made from 1 pound (450 grams) of dried apricots, soaked for twelve hours, then cut up; add more water and ferment with a little sugar on the pulp for two days before straining and finishing in the jar.

Blackberry wine

blackberries	6 pounds	*2.5 kilograms*
sugar	2½ pounds	*1 kilogram*
yeast, water		

Blackberries contain a good deal of juice so try 6 pints (3.5 litres) of boiling water for a start. Mash the fruit up in the bucket before pouring on the water. Infuse for four or five days, stirring and squeezing daily, then strain, put the juice in a jar and add the sugar and yeast. Add more cool boiled water if necessary. Ferment to a finish as usual.

Blackberry wine II

blackberries	4 pounds	*1.8 kilograms*
sugar	3–3½ pounds	*1.3–1.5 kilograms*
raisins (chopped)	4 ounces	*115 grams*
juice of 1 lemon		
cupful of strong tea		
yeast, water		

This wine is fermented on the pulp for three days. Put the fruit in a bucket and mash it well. Add the raisins and pour on the boiling water. When it has cooled to blood heat, stir in 1 pound (450 grams) of the sugar, the tea and the yeast. Port yeast is a good choice here. Stir daily for three days, keeping the bucket closely covered in between, then strain the must thoroughly and put it in a jar, adding the lemon juice. Either add the remainder of the sugar now, or a further pound (450 grams) now and the rest after a week. This should ferment out to a richly coloured, strong dessert wine, not unlike port.

Blackcurrant wine

blackcurrants	4 pounds	*1.8 kilograms*
sugar	3 pounds	*1.4 kilograms*
yeast, water		

This wine is made in the simplest way with an infusion, stirring and pressing well daily for five or six days, and then fermentation in a jar under airlock as usual.

Blackcurrant wine II

This old recipe makes a very powerful drink. Port yeast would seem appropriate.

blackcurrants	4 pounds	*1.8 kilograms*
sugar	3 pounds	*1.4 kilograms*
clear honey	8 ounces	*225 grams*
yeast, water		

Simmer the fruit in a large pan with 6 pints (3.5 litres) of water for fifteen minutes. Strain into a bucket and stir in the honey while it is still hot. (Solid honey can be liquefied by standing it in the airing cupboard or a pan of hot water for a while, but will anyway dissolve rapidly in boiling juice.) When it has cooled sufficiently, pour the juice into a jar and add the sugar and yeast. Fermentation may be violent at first so do not top up the jar at once, to avoid loss. Wait until it settles down. Ferment to a finish. My aunt used to top this up with brandy after racking it off for storage. It prevents any further fermentation and produces a potent drink to be drunk sparingly. Keep six months before bottling, then a further three to six months, if you can.

Cherry wine

Sweet cherries are seldom grown in modern gardens as the trees are large and the birds usually strip the fruit, and cherries are never cheap enough to buy for winemaking. However, the prolific cooking cherry called Morello is less subject to bird depredation and can be grown in a small garden, especially fan-trained on a fence or wall. It even thrives on a north-facing wall.

Morello cherries	4 pounds	*1.8 kilograms*
sugar	3 pounds	*1.4 kilograms*
yeast, water		

Infuse the fruit in boiling water and leave for seven days. The fruit is firm, so needs pressing well to release the juice. Proceed in the usual way. It was formerly a country custom to remove the stones from the strained Morello pulp, sweeten it and use it in pies. If sweet cherries are available, white or black, the same recipe can be used with 2¼ pounds (1 kilogram) of sugar. A mixture of 2 pounds (0.9 kilograms) each of black cherries and Morellos yields a good wine with a fine colour.

41

Damson wine

ripe damsons	4 pounds	*1.8 kilograms*
sugar	3 pounds	*1.4 kilograms*
yeast, water		

Infuse the fruit with boiling water in the usual way for five or six days, pressing and stirring well. Ferment in the usual way.

Double damson wine

damsons	4 pounds	*1.8 kilograms*
sugar	5½ pounds	*2.5 kilograms*
raisins	1 pound	*450 grams*
juice of 1 lemon		
cupful of strong tea		
yeast, water		

Two jars will be needed and double quantities of yeast and water as this recipe makes two different wines. Divide the sugar into two lots, 3½ pounds (1.6 kilograms) for jar A, 2 pounds (0.9 kilograms) for jar B. Put the prepared fruit into the bucket and pour on sufficient boiling water to make 1 gallon (4.5 litres) of wine. 6 pints (3.5 litres) is probably enough. Ferment this by the on-pulp method. When the water has cooled sufficiently add some of the sugar from lot A and yeast (a port yeast perhaps) and allow it to ferment for three or four days. Strain off the juice, put it in a jar, add the rest of the lot A sugar, and ferment under an airlock in the usual way.

Do not discard the strained pulp but replace it in the bucket. Add the raisins, chopped or minced, the lemon juice and tea, and pour over a further quantity of boiling water, then stir in the lot B sugar. Ferment this must with an all-purpose wine yeast for three days on the pulp, then strain it and put into the second jar. Fit an airlock and proceed as usual. This will yield a dryish table wine, very different from the robust first jar.

Elderberry wine

This is a traditional favourite, at its best a great country wine. The berries are rich in tannin so do not add any or use too much fruit. Try to use well ripened fruit; too many unripe berries can give a very harsh taste, though this will smooth out as the wine matures. A fork can be used to strip the berries from the stems. A Burgundy yeast is often used to make this wine.

elderberries	4 pounds	*1.8 kilograms*
sugar (Demerara is good)	2½ pounds	*1.2 kilograms*

raisins	8 ounces	*225 grams*
root ginger (crushed)	1 ounce	*28 grams*
yeast, water		

Pour boiling water over the berries, raisins and bruised ginger, crush well and leave to infuse for six days, stirring often. Strain over the sugar in a sterilised jar, add yeast and ferment as usual.

Some people prefer to ferment this on the pulp for three days, not longer, in which case add 1 pound (450 grams) of sugar and the yeast when the water has cooled to blood heat, and the remainder of the sugar when transferring the strained must to the jar. Ferment to a finish and keep in a storage jar for at least twelve months, and for a further three after bottling.

Sweet elderberry wine
Increase the sugar to $3\frac{1}{2}$ pounds (1.6 kilograms) and if you like use a port yeast. Another version adds six cloves to the infusion or even in the jar. A sherry glassful of brandy used often to be added before closing down for storage.

Light elderberry wine
elderberries	$2\frac{1}{2}$ pounds	*1.2 kilograms*
sugar	2 pounds	*0.9 kilograms*
yeast, water		

Use either the infusion or the on-pulp method. Fasten down when fermentation stops and bottle as soon as it clears. This is a dry table wine which needs no long maturing time as other elderberry wines do. It can be drunk quite soon.

Elderberry wine II
elderberries	4 pounds	*1.8 kilograms*
sugar	$3\frac{1}{2}$ pounds	*1.6 kilograms*
root ginger	1 ounce	*28 grams*
6 cloves		
1 lemon		
yeast, water		

Infuse the berries in boiling water in the usual way. Leave for three days, crushing and stirring well. Strain the juice into a pan and add the thinly peeled rind of the lemon, the well bruised root ginger and the cloves. Bring it to the boil, simmer for ten minutes and allow to cool. Strain and pour the juice into a jar with the sugar, the lemon juice and the yeast. Ferment to a finish. Orange peel and juice can be used as flavouring instead.

Gooseberry wine

gooseberries	4 pounds	*1.8 kilograms*
sugar	3 pounds	*1.4 kilograms*
root ginger	1 ounce	*28 grams*
yeast, water		

Infuse and ferment this by the usual method, allowing five or six days for the infusion.

Unripe fruit imparts very little gooseberry flavour to the wine. Ripe gooseberries are best used for a sweet fruity wine, and green ones for a dry wine using 2½ pounds (1.2 kilograms) of sugar. Green gooseberries make a pleasant sparkling wine if you can judge when to bottle it, but note the remarks on pages 60–1. This wine often starts a gentle secondary fermentation. I have had several batches which were hardly sparkling but had a delightful and entirely natural prickle – what is sometimes described as 'starry'.

Grape wine

Grapes are the stuff of which 'real' wine is made but no water or sugar is used because the juice of grapes ripened under the right conditions contains the ideal proportions of natural sugar, acid, tannin and flavour. Vineyards flourished in Britain centuries ago and some have been established in recent years. At least two in Hampshire bottle wine commercially. The choice of grape and site is critical and proper pruning is important. Those interested should read a book such as *Wine Growing in England* by George Ordich (Hart-Davis), available at public libraries.

Many people grow a vine on the house wall or pergola or in a cold greenhouse, and though the grapes may not make much size or get enough sun to develop and ripen quite as they should, they will still make good wine. Black or green grapes can be used: the former will give a red wine of less intense colour than a commercial red wine because the fruit is diluted with water and sugar as the wine is made like other country wines and is not just fermented juice.

grapes	4 pounds	*1.8 kilograms*
sugar	3 pounds	*1.4 kilograms*
yeast, water		

Crush the fruit in the bucket, pour on the boiling water and infuse for five or six days, then proceed as usual. Use 2 pounds (0.9 kilograms) of sugar for a drier wine, 3½–4 pounds (1.6–1.8 kilograms) for a sweeter one. Grapes in Britain can be rather tasteless but a variety of flavours can be obtained with the addition of other fruits, even in small quantities. A few black-berries will give a richer colour to red wine, and raisins (only dried grapes really) will add body. There are many other possibilities.

Haw wine and hip wine

These wild fruits are often available in large quantities and free. Haws are high in tannin and I prefer not to use them alone in wine. The hips from wild or garden roses can be used alone, or with haws. Hips are best cut in half before soaking, but both these fruits are hard and need a lot of pressing to extract the flavour.

hips and/or haws	4 pounds	*1.8 kilograms*
sugar	2½–3 pounds	*1.2–1.4 kilograms*
juice of 2 lemons		
yeast, water		

Crush the fruit well and pour on the boiling water. Infuse for six days, then ferment in a jar with the sugar, lemon juice and yeast in the usual way.

Loganberry wine

loganberries	4 pounds	*1.8 kilograms*
sugar	3½ pounds	*1.6 kilograms*
yeast, water		

Infuse for four days in boiling water, stirring and pressing well. Strain and ferment in the usual way. If fruit is scarce, a pleasant drier wine can be made using 2½ pounds (1.1 kilograms) of loganberries, the same of sugar, and 8 ounces (225 grams) of chopped raisins. Using honey in place of some of the sugar gives a special flavour to loganberry wine.

Mulberry wine

I never see mulberries on sale but there is no problem in obtaining them if you have a tree, or know someone who has, as crops are usually enormous. In my childhood, the method was to spread old clean sheets under the tree and as the birds helped themselves from the branches above, ten times as many berries rained down and only needed collecting. Use a bucket for this, not a basket, as juice drips through and it stains clothing indelibly. Offer a couple of bottles of wine in exchange for surplus fruit if you can locate a tree.

Use a loganberry wine recipe.

Orange wine
Though hardly a native fruit, oranges are sometimes available cheaply. Do not forget to clean the skins thoroughly before using them. There is some argument about whether oranges can be used entirely, or whether the pith should be discarded after the rind has been thinly peeled, and the segments separated. I have tasted wine made by slicing the whole fruit, by using only peel and segments, and by treating half each way. All tasted different but all were good and none was bitter. So suit yourself! Half Seville and half sweet oranges may be used.

12 oranges		
raisins	1 pound	*450 grams*
sugar	2½ pounds	*1.1 kilograms*
cupful of strong tea		
yeast, water		

Slice or otherwise prepare the oranges and put them with the raisins, chopped, into a bucket. Pour over them the boiling water and infuse for four days, crushing and stirring frequently. Strain and place in a jar with the sugar, tea and yeast. Alternatively ferment on the pulp with 1 pound (450 grams) of sugar for three days before straining and transferring to a jar with the rest of the sugar and continuing fermentation to a finish.

Orange wine II
The following recipe was given me by a lady who let me taste her very pleasant wine.

unsweetened orange juice	1 pint	*600 millilitres*
sugar	2–3 pounds	*0.9–1.4 kilograms*
yeast and nutrient, water		

Put the juice in a jar with 2 pounds (0.9 kilograms) of sugar, the yeast and yeast nutrient, and 4 pints (2.3 litres) of boiled water cooled to blood heat. If you want a dry wine, top up the jar with more cool boiled water; if a sweeter one, add a further 1 pound (460 grams) of sugar made into a syrup, when the fermentation has settled down. More orange juice may be used at the start, and various different yeasts. This is a very simple wine which would lend itself to experiment.

Orange (Seville) wine

12 Seville oranges		
sugar	4 pounds	*1.8 kilograms*
2 lemons		
yeast, water		

Peel half the oranges and throw away the rinds. Slice up the fruit and also the six unpeeled oranges and the lemons. Put them into a bucket, pour on the boiling water and infuse for fourteen days, adding the yeast as soon as it cools sufficiently, and stirring daily. At the end of this time strain the juice, put in the sugar and stir well to dissolve it, then pour into a sterilised jar and ferment under an airlock. If there is any surplus juice, put it in a dark bottle, to preserve the colour, and plug with cotton wool: it will continue fermenting and can be used to top up the jar. Ferment to a finish, fasten down the jar and rack into a clean one when it has cleared. Leave for at least two months after this before bottling.

Peach wine

Peaches grow well in some parts of Britain and can produce a glut.

peaches	5 pounds	*2.3 kilograms*
sugar	2½ pounds	*1.1 kilograms*
1 lemon, 2 oranges		
yeast, water		

Cut up the peaches and discard the stones. Put the fruit in a bucket and add the thinly peeled rind of the citrus fruits, then pour in the boiling water. Infuse for four or five days, stirring and pressing the fruit daily, then strain and proceed as usual.

Pear wine

pears	4 pounds	*1.8 kilograms*
sugar	3 pounds	*1.4 kilograms*
juice of 2 lemons		
yeast, water		

The method is as for apple wine. If the pears are rather tasteless, try ginger root in the infusion. I have tasted a very good pear wine made with a hock yeast.

Plum wine

ripe plums	4 pounds	*1.8 kilograms*
sugar	3 pounds	*1.4 kilograms*
yeast, water		

The method is as for damson wine.

Plum port

This powerful drink was offered me by an elderly lady who used 4 pounds (1.8 kilograms) of 'blue' plums to 3½ pounds (1.6

kilograms) of sugar to produce a strong sweet wine, to which she added a gill (0.1 litres) of brandy when she racked it off. She insisted that it needed eighteen months in the jar before bottling, and to be drunk with respect!

Quince wine

Few gardens have a quince tree, though it is small, useful and ornamental and could well replace monotonous flowering cherries. However the Japanese quince (*Cydonia* or *Chaenomeles*), often called japonica, is widely grown as a garden shrub and its abundant fruit is frequently wasted. It makes good wine (as well as delicious jelly) but the fragrant fruits are so hard they must be boiled; and so much pectin is released that the wine is hard to clear. A pectin-degrading enzyme will correct this.

quinces	4 pounds	*1.8 kilograms*
sugar	2½ pounds	*1.1 kilograms*
juice of 1 lemon		
1 orange		
yeast, pectic enzyme, water		

Chop up the quinces and put them in a large saucepan with the thinly peeled rind of the orange, cover with water, bring to the boil and simmer for fifteen minutes. Strain into a bucket and when the liquid has cooled to blood heat pour it into a jar. Add the sugar, fruit juices, yeast and pectic enzyme. Ferment to a finish. This wine is especially delightful if honey is used in place of some of the sugar.

Raspberry wine

raspberries	4 pounds	*1.8 kilograms*
sugar	3 pounds	*1.4 kilograms*
yeast, water		

Mash the raspberries well in the bucket before pouring the boiling water over them. Stir daily for four days before straining off the liquid and putting it into a jar. Add the sugar and yeast and proceed as usual. Some winemakers recommend a sherry yeast for raspberry wine.

Rhubarb wine

This is a favourite of mine as it lends itself to endless variation. Every winemaker acquires a collection of recipes for rhubarb wine, although it has a reputation for adversely affecting folk with rheumatism. Late-season rhubarb becomes watery and acid with little flavour, so do not leave it too long.

rhubarb	4–5 pounds	*1.8–2.2 kilograms*
sugar	2½ pounds	*1.1 kilograms*
juice of 2 oranges		
yeast, water		

Cut up the sticks, put them in a bucket and crush well. My old wooden potato masher is fine for this. Pour on the boiling water and stir and press daily for five days. Strain and add the liquid to the sugar, orange juice and yeast in a sterilised jar, and ferment in the usual way under an airlock.

Sweet rhubarb wine

rhubarb	5 pounds	*2.2 kilograms*
sugar	3½ pounds	*1.6 kilograms*
raisins	8 ounces	*225 grams*
1 lemon		
yeast, water		

Chop rhubarb and raisins and place in a bucket with the thinly pared lemon rind. Pour on the boiling water and leave for five or six days, stirring and pressing daily. Strain off the liquid and ferment with the sugar, lemon juice and yeast in the usual way. All or part of the sugar may be Demerara, which will give a richer flavour and colour.

Quick rhubarb wine

rhubarb	3–4 pounds	*1.4–1.8 kilograms*
sugar	3 pounds	*1.4 kilograms*
cupful of strong tea		
yeast, water		

Slice the rhubarb thinly, put it in a bucket and cover it with the sugar, but *no water*. Cover well and leave for two days. There will be a lot of liquid, which you pour off carefully into a sterilised jar. To the pulp in the bucket add boiling water. The amount depends on what juice you have already obtained, but try perhaps 5 pints (2.8 litres) as you can top it up later. Stir the pulp well and when it has cooled strain off the liquid and add it to the jar. Add the tea and the yeast and ferment as usual. This light wine matures quickly and can be drunk soon after it clears.

Rowan wine

As rowan berries are high in tannin and astringent in flavour, use 1–2 pounds (0.5–1 kilogram) to 3 pounds (1.4 kilograms) of sugar. If fermented on the pulp it should be for no more than three days. They could also be mixed with rosehips and haws for an autumn wine.

Sloe wine

sloes	3½ pounds	*1.6 kilograms*
sugar	3¼ pounds	*1.5 kilograms*
yeast, water		

Put the sloes (complete with stones) into a bucket and pour over them 5 pints (3 litres) of boiling water. Infuse the fruit, stirring and pressing daily, for four days, then strain it. Put the juice into a jar with 1½ pounds (680 grams) of sugar and the yeast. After three days of fermentation add a further 1¾ pints(1 litre) of water and 8 ounces (226 grams) of sugar made into syrup. Make sure this is as warm as the must to which you are adding it, to prevent a check to fermentation. Two months later add the remaining sugar and continue the fermentation until complete. Fasten down and keep at least twelve months before bottling, racking as necessary.

Mixed fruit wines

Mixed fruit wines offer unlimited scope for experiment. They are ideal for using a small quantity of fruit which will not make a full jar, or for making several different wines from a glut of one fruit. The proportions may be half and half or any other. Some blackberries might be added to an apple wine to give a rosé colour and different taste, or some elderberries to a blackberry wine to give additional bite. Dates or cheap over-ripe bananas will add body and sweetness to something which might otherwise be rather thin and astringent. Nor need you limit yourself to two fruits. An autumn mixture of hips, haws and rowanberries has been mentioned, but this could benefit from the inclusion of blackberries and elderberries also. Having for years made a Summer Medley jam from gooseberries, raspberries, strawberries and loganberries I can see no reason why a wine on the same lines should not be equally successful. Apples and rhubarb are good basics with which scarcer or more expensive fruits, or exotic imported ones, can be mixed. Do keep a note of the ingredients you use and the quantities, so that you can repeat or adjust them another time.

Among the mixed fruit wines which I have made successfully or tasted with pleasure are the following: apple and blackberry; apple and grape; apple and pear; blackcurrant and redcurrant; blackberry and elderberry; damson and greengage; orange and raisin; plum and damson; raspberry and mulberry; rhubarb and (overwintered) apple; rhubarb and banana; rhubarb and blackberry; rhubarb and fig; rhubarb and raspberry; but the possibilities are limitless.

6. Vegetable and cereal wines

Vegetables, especially roots, can yield a considerable surplus in even a small garden and have been turned into wine by generations of country folk, although in some ways they are scarcely ideal. Many, from sugarbeet down, have a high sugar content so the amount added should be carefully controlled. Vegetable wines are sickly if they are too sweet because they lack acid and tannin. These are usually added in the shape of fruit juices and tea, or citric acid crystals and grape tannin, according to choice. Try the juice of two citrus fruits and a cupful (up to $\frac{1}{2}$ pint or 280 millilitres) of freshly made strong tea, or one heaped teaspoonful of citric acid and a saltspoonful of tannin, as a starting point. Vegetables are rather hard so recipes often call for boiling them. This releases starch which can persist as a haze in the finished wine. However, all my vegetable wines have cleared perfectly, given time, without recourse to artificial remedies. They are, in general, wines for keeping, not for consumption after three or four months in store. While many splendid and potent beverages are made from vegetables, and good parsnip wine is rightly regarded as a classic, claims about wheat or potato 'whisky' and carrot wine 'exactly like sherry' must be treated with scepticism. No country wine can achieve the equivalent alcoholic content unless it is fortified with spirits and even then would scarcely taste the same. And why should it? Why not enjoy a good carrot wine as itself rather than as pseudo-Amontillado?

There is no doubt that in the past vegetables used for winemaking were also eaten, though not where on-pulp fermentation was carried out. This pulp, when discarded, was often eaten by farm livestock and tales are told of drunken pigs and inebriated poultry staggering about the farmyard after feasting on such treasure trove. I know a certain country housewife who used to make a wine from beetroot and parsnips, which were boiled separately. The smallest beets were used whole, walnut to ping-pong-ball size, and after boiling and straining off the juice for wine they were peeled, packed in jars and covered with spiced vinegar. The parsnip chunks after cooking and straining went into the stew or were mashed with butter, salt and pepper and used as a vegetable or to top a cottage pie. The two batches of juice were combined and fermented with tea, lemon juice and sugar into a pleasant wine. This is real rural economy! Elsewhere I have mentioned Morello cherries being used in pies after an initial infusion and – dried fruits being now so expensive – I have a feeling a proper country housewife would find some way of saving and reusing raisins from the wine

51

bucket. Providing the vegetables are well scrubbed (not peeled) and bad portions cut out, there can be no objection to using them up. They should not be overcooked, *never* to a mush, but simmered gently until just tender. Old tough vegetables would not be palatable although they will make good wine, and in this case any additions such as crushed root ginger and lemon and orange rind can be boiled with them.

Cereals can be bought but are not so readily available free. If you can get permission from a farmer to glean in a wheat field after the combine harvester has done its work and before the stubble is burnt (or the birds have cleared up) an amazing quantity of grain can be found. Children are good at gleaning, being small-fingered and close to the ground. If you buy grain from a corn merchant or pet-food shop, wash it well as it may contain grit, floor sweepings and mouse droppings.

General instructions

Vegetable wines may be made by the infusion method, or the vegetables may be cooked and the juice strained off. Starch haze may be more of a problem if the material is cooked. Prepare the vegetables carefully, put them in a bucket and pour over them sufficient boiling water. Keep the bucket closely covered. Stir and press well daily. Strain the liquid off. If cooking the vegetables, strain, but allow to cool before proceeding. Pour the liquid into a warm jar, add other ingredients and fit an airlock. If preferred, fermentation can be started in the bucket and continued for three days. When filled, label the jar and keep it in a warm place, shielded from light. Mop up any spills as soon as possible. Keep the airlock clean and do not allow water to evaporate from it. If you wish to add the sugar in instalments, especially as syrup, remember to leave space for it, and keep a note of the date and amount. When fermentation ceases, top up the jar and close it with a sterilised cork. Put away in a cool dark place.

In the following recipes yeast may be the special wine yeast of your choice or an all-purpose wine yeast, used according to the maker's instructions, or half of a 1 ounce (28 gram) packet of dried baker's yeast. It is your own choice whether you add yeast nutrient or not. Water means enough to make 1 gallon (4.5 litres) of wine: less must be used for the initial boiling or infusion if you wish to add the yeast as an already active starter or part of the sugar as syrup at a later stage. Cool boiled water can be used to top up the jar when necessary. If peel of citrus fruits is to be included in a recipe, remember to clean the skins thoroughly by dunking the fruit in a pan of boiling water a few times.

Beetroot wine

raw beetroot	4 pounds	1.8 kilograms
sugar	2 pounds	0.9 kilograms
root ginger	1 ounce	28 grams
juice of 2 lemons		
cupful of strong tea		
yeast, water		

Wash and slice the beetroot, put it in the bucket with the root ginger (crushed), and pour over it the boiling water. Leave it to infuse for four days, stirring and pressing daily. Strain off the liquid and put it into a jar with the sugar, lemon juice, tea and yeast and ferment to a finish under an airlock. If there is much sediment, rack off into a clean jar and fasten down; if not, cork it down and leave in a cool place to start clearing, then rack off later.

The harsh colour of beetroot is not wine-red and looks un-appetising to my eyes but it does mellow to a less aggressive tawny red. Boiling the vegetable might produce a still stronger colour so I have not tried that method.

Carrot wine

raw carrots	4 pounds	1.8 kilograms
sugar	2–2½ pounds	0.9–1.1 kilograms
juice of 1 lemon, 1 orange		
cupful of strong tea		
yeast, water		

Use the same method as for beetroot wine.

Carrot wine II

carrots	5 pounds	2.3 kilograms
sugar	2½ pounds	1.1 kilograms
raisins	8 ounces	225 grams
2 oranges		
cupful of tea		
yeast, water		

Simmer the carrots, cut into chunks, in a large pan with the raisins and some of the orange rind, thinly peeled, for about twenty minutes. Strain off the liquid into a bucket and when it has cooled transfer it to the jar with the sugar, the juice of the oranges, the tea and the yeast. Ferment in the usual way. The longer this is kept in the jar before bottling the better it is.

Marrow wine

marrow	6 pounds	2.7 kilograms
sugar	3 pounds	1.4 kilograms
root ginger	1 ounce	28 grams
juice of 3 lemons		
yeast, water		

Wash the marrow and cut it all up. Include the peel, seeds and flesh. Add to it the crushed ginger root and pour on the boiling water. Infuse for six days, pressing and stirring daily. Strain and put into a jar with the sugar, juice and yeast, and ferment to a finish. Demerara sugar gives this wine a better colour and flavour.

Parsnip wine

Parsnips should not be used until after the autumn frosts have sweetened them, or so country people have always insisted.

parsnips	4 pounds	1.8 kilograms
brown sugar (Demerara)	3 pounds	1.4 kilograms
1 lemon		
cupful of tea		
yeast, water		

Scrub and trim the parsnips and cut them up. Infuse them with the thinly peeled lemon rind for five days, or simmer vegetable and rind together in a saucepan with the water for ten to fifteen minutes, then strain. Put the liquid into a jar with the sugar, lemon juice and yeast. Parsnip wine is usually made in cold weather and it is important to ensure a sufficiently high *constant* temperature to maintain a brisk fermentation. Like other root wines this needs to be kept in bulk as long as possible. Three or four years is not too long.

Peapod wine

peapods (empty)	5 pounds	2.3 kilograms
sugar	3 pounds	1.4 kilograms
juice of 1 lemon, 1 orange		
yeast, water		

Pour the boiling water over the peapods in a bucket and infuse, stirring daily, for four days. Strain off the liquid and put it in a jar with the sugar, fruit juices and yeast. Ferment to a finish.

Potato wine

potatoes	4 pounds	*1.8 kilograms*
sugar	2 pounds	*0.9 kilograms*
raisins	4 ounces	*115 grams*
pearl barley	8 ounces	*225 grams*
juice of 1 lemon, 1 orange		
cupful of strong tea		
yeast, water		

Scrub the potatoes well, and slice them thinly. Put them in a bucket with the barley and raisins, pour on boiling water and infuse for four days, stirring daily. Strain off the liquid and put it into a jar with the sugar, fruit juices, tea and yeast and ferment to a finish.

Potato wine II

potatoes	5 pounds	*2.3 kilograms*
brown sugar (Demerara)	3 pounds	*1.4 kilograms*
root ginger	1 ounce	*28 grams*
juice of 2 lemons,		
1 orange		
cupful of strong tea		
yeast, water		

Scrub and cut up the potatoes and put them in a saucepan with the water. Bring to the boil and simmer for two or three minutes, then tip into a bucket, stir in the ginger, well crushed, and infuse for four days. Strain the liquid into a jar and add the sugar, fruit juices, tea and yeast. Ferment as usual.

Wheat wine

wheat	1 pint	*0.5 litres*
raisins	2 pounds	*0.9 kilograms*
sugar	3½ pounds	*1.6 kilograms*
yeast, water		

Pour boiling water over the wheat, chopped raisins and sugar in a bucket. Stir thoroughly and allow to cool, then add the yeast. Keep closely covered while fermenting for three weeks on the pulp, then strain into the jar and continue the fermentation under an airlock. After completion, cork down and store. Rack as necessary but do not bottle for a year.

This may be a good place to give some rather odd wines which do not fit into any category, namely tea and coffee wines. Tea wine, made in many different ways, is a very well established favourite and must have been evolved as a way of using any precious 'leftovers' when tea was both scarce and expensive. Some tea wines I have tasted – and made – were rather nasty but the following recipe gave a good result. Coffee wine must be of much more recent date but shows a commendable urge to experiment.

Tea wine

cold tea	1 gallon approx.	*4.5 litres*
raisins	1 pound	*450 grams*
sugar	3–3½ pounds	*1.4–1.6 kilograms*
juice of 2 lemons		
yeast, water		

Undoubtedly tea wine was made in the past from the cold tea left in the pot, strained, and saved until there was enough for a gallon (4.5 litres) of wine. It could be made from freshly brewed tea if you prefer. In either case the tea should be poured hot over the chopped raisins in a bucket. Stir well. When cooled to blood heat, add the lemon juice and yeast, and ferment on the pulp for six days. Strain off the liquid, squeezing the raisins to extract as much juice as possible, and put it into a jar with 1 pound (450 grams) of sugar, adding the rest at intervals (keep a note of the dates and amounts) to prolong the fermentation. When it is complete, close the jar and keep the wine for at least six months before bottling it. It makes a pleasant drink with which to end a meal.

Coffee wine

ground coffee	8 ounces	*225 grams*
sugar	3–3½ pounds	*1.4–1.6 kilograms*
raisins	8 ounces	*225 grams*
juice of 2 lemons *or*		
1 lemon, 1 orange		
yeast, water		

Instant coffee could be used instead of ground. Save or make freshly about 7 pints (4 litres) of coffee and pour it boiling hot over the chopped raisins in a bucket. Stir well, then add the lemon juice and 1 pound (450 grams) of sugar and stir again. When it is cool enough, add the yeast. Twenty-four hours later, when the fermentation has started, strain the liquid and put it in a warm jar. Fit an airlock and continue fermentation, adding the rest of the sugar in two instalments at intervals of two to three weeks. Store for at least six months before bottling. If this is made with part or all brown sugar, the result can be an after-dinner drink a little like a coffee liqueur, although it has not the alcoholic content.

7. Things which can go wrong

Vinegar bug

This is impossible to cure, though with normal care it should never occur. The vinegary smell and taste are unmistakable when it does. The addition of one or two crushed Campden tablets will kill the 'bug' and prevent further action but will also kill the yeast and arrest fermentation. A certain amount of unconverted sugar would remain as well as the vinegary taste. I have not tried, but perhaps it could be left to turn into vinegar and used to make pickles?

Mould on pulp

This mould, which can form on the surface of an on-pulp fermentation or on the soaking materials before the ferment is started, may look revolting, but a great many recipes which were used for generations assume that this mould would form, even telling the reader to wait until it does and giving instructions for removing it, which was done. So do not panic. Remove it as carefully as you can with a spoon before straining the juice, and proceed with the fermentation. I once forgot some soaking apple pulp, which formed a blue-green crust, to my horror, but I continued in this way, in a spirit of scientific enquiry, and produced one of the best apple wines ever. A very advanced winemaker of my acquaintance thinks our ancestors may have been right and the mould may impart a beneficial extra something to the wine. Stranger things have been proved correct. However, a brisk daily stir, or even a plate or some such laid on top of the pulp to hold it below the liquid, will usually prevent this happening. If you decide to add a crushed Campden tablet to sterilise the juice, leave it at least twenty-four hours and then disperse the sulphite with a brisk stir before adding your yeast, or its development could be inhibited.

Pectin haze

This is a condition in which wine fails to clear because the tiny globules of jelly it contains hold minute solids in suspension, instead of allowing them to drop to the bottom as sediment. It is commonest in fruit wines, especially when the fruit is cooked or there is a long on-pulp fermentation. It has not occurred in any wine I have made by the infusion of soft fruits, but a (cooked) quince wine remained cloudy. The taste is not spoilt but the appearance is unsatisfactory. Nowadays pectin-degrading enzyme is available with names like Pectinol and Pectolase. If it seems necessary, this should be added according to the maker's directions when the juice is cool. The most convenient time is when adding the yeast and sugar. If you have not used it and a fruit wine subsequently shows no sign of clearing within a reasonable period, the enzyme can be added while racking off and will disperse it successfully.

Starch haze

This happens less frequently and is a defect found only in cereal and root vegetable wines. I believe it would eventually clear, given time, but it could be a long time. If your patience is exhausted you can buy something called fungal amylase and use it according to instructions. It is easiest to do this when racking off the wine. The fungal amylase is mixed into a small quantity of wine, placed in a fresh sterilised jar, and the remainder of the wine is siphoned in on top. This avoids the messy business of trying to ensure an even distribution throughout the jar by stirring.

Unused yeast

I have several times seen grey-white lumps floating about in wine which the novice winemaker fondly imagined had completed its fermentation, but this was yeast which had never really begun to ferment. Usually the trouble is temperature. For a good ferment warmth is essential and it should be constant within a degree or two. A good start is vital; and this requires a warm jar and warm must to add the yeast to, especially if it is in the form of an already working starter which could be stopped in its tracks by sudden immersion in a jar of cold juice. The cure for this condition is to move the jar to a warm place, fit an airlock and get a good fermentation going. If stored, a sudden heatwave could well start a fermentation brisk enough to blow out the cork or burst the jar.

Stuck fermentation

As mentioned above, low temperature is the most frequent cause of sluggish fermentation. The problem is less acute in summer but even in warm weather a sunless concrete garage built on the north side of the house will not provide suitable conditions for fermenting wine. Such places strike a chill to one's own skin on the hottest day. Too high a temperature is less likely but can also stop fermentation. At 38C (100F) the yeast organism is killed. Oxygen starvation may also slow or stop fermentation, which is why it often puts on a new spurt when the wine is racked off – it gets a breath of fresh air. A brisk stir would have the same effect. Stale yeast is another cause of a poor fermentation. If it has been in stock for a long time you could try adding a little more fresh yeast. If you like you could put in a teaspoonful of yeast nutrient but do not be tempted to add more from time to time with the idea of 'waking it up'. A lot of wine is spoilt by tinkering about with it, adding a teaspoonful of yeast, another pinch of nutrient or a scrap more sugar because the ferment seems to be flagging or slower than expected. Get it away to a good start and leave it alone.

Hot tangy taste

This is probably oxidation resulting from overexposure to the air. It is prevented by keeping containers full, using airlocks, and careful non-splashy racking and bottling. Once there, it is irreversible. Other odd tastes may result from using metal containers or lead-glazed earthenware ones, or lack of attention to cleanliness.

Too dry wine

You can sweeten wine that is too dry. Long ago a judge wrote on my card that the elderflower wine I had entered in a show was too dry and suggested I add sugar. 'How?' I asked myself in my ignorance. Surely it would not dissolve in cold wine. So I would heat it. It was late by the time I had unpacked and eaten a meal but I wanted to try it before going to bed. I heated the wine in a saucepan, not quite to boiling, added sugar and (with memories of my mother doing likewise) a shake of cinnamon, put it in a tankard and sat down to savour the brew. It was much improved. I awoke at 3 a.m. after a deep refreshing sleep but a trifle chilled! Apart from making mulled wine, you *can* sweeten wine. Pour a quarter of the bottle into a jug or beaker, glass or china, stir in two teaspoonfuls of sugar, then heat it by standing the jug in hot water over a low flame just until the sugar dissolves. Return it to the bottle, mix well, then taste it. Repeat the process if necessary. Once it tastes right to you, treat the remainder of the batch in the same proportions. If it has been bottled, it is best to return the whole sweetened gallon (4.5 litres) to a jar and fix an airlock in case the extra sugar starts it fermenting again. You could add one crushed Campden tablet if you want to fasten it down at once, since this will ensure that no live yeast remains.

Too sweet wine

This is less easy to deal with. If the trouble is an unsatisfactory ferment which has left too much unconverted sugar and a low alcohol content so that it tastes syrupy, you could add an active starter and begin again. Otherwise blending is the answer.

Blending

Blending can cope with many wine problems as well as oversweet wines, among them the too dry, too acid or insipid ones. It is great fun but you need to have made wine for some years in order to have a diverse collection of many different kinds. As a general rule, flower wines of distinctive flavour and bouquet do not blend well together, though they will with an apple or rhubarb wine of suitable type. Fruit wines usually blend satisfactorily. It is customary to say that red fruit wines should only be blended with other reds, and whites with whites. I love rosé wines, which are pretty and eminently suitable for consuming sociably in the garden on summer afternoons in comfortable chairs, and I can see no objection to mixing a red and a white wine together to produce a rosé, providing the flavours blend well. Root wines blend satisfactorily, but often better still with those made from oranges or lemons. However, there are no unbreakable rules and you may discover something marvellous by experiment.

The main thing is to taste the wine you have, *really* taste it. We all like drinking wine but there is more to it than simply swallowing it down, just as there is more to blending than sloshing wine from one bottle into another and hoping for the best. You must taste your wine with your mind, assessing not only its sweetness or dryness but its acidity, body and astringency, and trying to analyse what it contains, perhaps to excess, and what it lacks. You must smell and sip it, let it run round in your mouth, concentrate on it with closed eyes. If you want to sample another after it, put it in a clean glass, not on the dregs of the former one, and eat – slowly – a piece of bread or cheese or a dry biscuit to cleanse the palate before you sniff the aroma and sip the new one.

You have, say, a very dry wine, rather acid, which you want to blend with another sweet, rather bland one. In what proportion? To decide this with any accuracy you need two small liquid measures, which will probably be marked in fluid ounces and millilitres. Begin by measuring an equal quantity of each variety in the separate glasses, then pour them together into a shining clean small wineglass, swirl the liquid round and taste it. Not quite right yet? Which do you need more of? Cleanse your palate, take a fresh wineglass and try again with a different proportion of each. Use as little as possible for each sample, to avoid waste. When you have arrived at a palatable blend, you can make up a larger amount in the same proportions and bottle it. Always pour it gently, and avoid exposure to the air for any longer than is necessary, when blending.

Blown corks

This is not a fault in winemaking except in so far as the fermentation was judged to be complete when it was not. In most cases the ferment has been arrested by a change of temperature and the still living yeast has remained inactive while the wine has been stored in a cold place. Sometimes it starts to work again because a jar of wine is brought into a warm kitchen for bottling, which stirs it up and provides fresh oxygen. This might do no more than impart a faint prickle to the wine but if it were sufficiently lively the new fermentation might generate enough gas to force out the corks. It is possible to wire on the corks and produce sparkling wine but a miscalculation in this case might mean exploding bottles rather than blown corks. It would be unlikely to come to that if the bottles were returned to a cold storage place after filling. However, bottles which have been in store for months sometimes blow out their corks because the winter cold which kept yeast dormant gives way to warmer summer weather which reactivates it. Regular inspections will reveal the cork which looks dark or sticky with seepage before it is blown out and the wine is wasted.

Storage faults

I have given some guidance elsewhere on this subject but many failures and losses are due to storing otherwise good wine unsuitably. The spacious chilly cellars of Victorian days have gone and few houses are left which have the cool north-facing stone-flagged larders, dairies and stillrooms considered essential before refrigerators became commonplace. If you have this kind of storage space you are fortunate, but modern homes are the majority and pose problems. The chilly north-facing concrete garage mentioned earlier as an unsuitable place for fermenting wine may well be ideal for storing it. The loft never is. It may be freezing cold in winter but the sun beating on the roof makes it stiflingly hot in summer. If there is insulation it is usually between the joists and does not affect the loft space. If the roof itself is well enough insulated to keep out the summer heat it will keep in the winter heat from the house below and may be too warm as heat rises. A coal shed on the sunless side of the house, made redundant by central heating, might be a good store. Corrugated iron roofs exposed to the sun convert the space below them into ovens but might be lined and insulated. The cupboard under the stairs is often chosen as it is dark and has no window and often no outside wall, so the temperature remains constant. I use such a cupboard which in my old house has its original solid brick floor. This keeps it cool with a tendency to damp. The latter is not harmful – the wine cellars of the Victorian house where I was born had walls often decorated with blue mould. The wine was none the worse for it, indeed it probably helped keep the corks tight. The air in centrally heated houses is often too drying, as

61

owners of antique furniture and troublesome sinuses find out.

Having found the constantly cool spot in which to keep them, bottles are stored horizontally or vertically according to the corks used (see page 12). Where wine racks are used, the front is usually raised a little above the horizontal by resting it on a batten, presumably to make them less likely to slide out if the rack is jolted. With the ends of the corks all presented to view, it is easy to spot seepage or a loosened cork in good time. I am often asked whether this condition would become obvious if flanged corks and viscose caps are used, and whether the cork would blow out or be held tight until the bottle burst. I do not use these corks myself but experts who do tell me that seeping wine will soften the cap, which can be seen by the vigilant, and will eventually loosen it and allow the cork to blow out if the pressure increases. With jars, corks can be pushed well in and, if there is a tendency for them to dry out during long storage, can be sealed with sealing wax. They will still blow out if conditions demand it. However, rubber bungs are a different matter. I would never use them for storage jars. For some reason, they adhere to the inside of the neck in a manner which makes them at times virtually impossible to remove. It seems to me that they could well resist a considerable pressure from within the jar and I would not care to have a jar exploding in my 'cellar'. It is also difficult to remove a fermentation lock from a pierced rubber bung after it has been there a while so I avoid them.

Wines do absorb tiny amounts of air through the corks. This helps to mature and improve the wine, and for this reason it is unwise to store wine in close proximity to onions, paraffin or any other strong-smelling commodity. People who have tried storing wine in plastic containers tell me the plastic absorbs any strong smell like this and can make the wine taste odd, so take extra care if you must use such containers.

Light affects the colour, especially of red and pink wines, which are traditionally bottled in dark glass bottles, though so too are some German white wines. Most experts agree that the taste is also affected, and that goes for white and golden wines too, so store everything in the dark. One wonders about the wines exposed to fluctuating temperatures and glaring light on supermarket shelves and in the windows of high-street wine-shops.

Appendix

Approximate equivalents

Alcoholic content by volume	Degrees proof spirit
4%	7
6%	$10^1/_2$
8%	14
10%	$17^1/_2$
12%	22
14%	$24^1/_2$
16%	28
18%	$31^1/_2$
20%	35
22%	$38^1/_2$
24%	42
26%	$45^1/_2$
28%	49
30%	52

and so on. 57.14% alcohol by volume is equal to 100 degrees proof spirit.

Index